How Living Wage Laws Affect Low-Wage Workers and Low-Income Families

• • •

David Neumark

2002

PUBLIC POLICY INSTITUTE OF CALIFORNIA

Library of Congress Cataloging-in-Publication Data
Neumark, David.
  How living wage laws affect low-wage workers and low-income
families / David Neumark.
    p. cm.
  Includes bibliographical references.
  ISBN 1-58213-043-4
    1. Living wage movement—United States. 2. Minimum
wage—United States. 3. Public contracts—United States.
4. Wages—Law and legislation—United States. 5. Cost and
standard of living—United States. 6. Households—United States.
7. Income—United States. 8. Poverty—United States. 9. Family
policy—United States. I. Title.

HD4973 .N48 2002
331.2'3—dc21   2001059607

Foreword

America's cities have traditionally pursued new development by providing a variety of economic incentives or subsidies to developers, investors, and landowners. Proponents of these subsidies argue that jobs and taxes stemming from the new growth more than compensate for the subsidy. However, in recent years, some city officials (influenced by labor and community organizations) have moved beyond the subject of job growth and have expressed concern about the adequacy of wages for those already employed.

The challenges facing a working-poor family in urban America are well documented, including housing availability and costs, health care, child care, and transportation. Thus, the concern in many cases has begun to focus on the quality of life among those at the lower end of the income distribution rather than on creating more jobs. National and state minimum wage laws are often viewed as too modest in their compensation, and thus various voices have called for a "living wage" that reflects the reality of living and working in today's urban centers.

In this study, Professor David Neumark, a visiting fellow at PPIC in 2001, takes a close look at living wage ordinances across the United States, assessing their effects on wage and employment levels of the urban poor and on urban poverty. Nationwide, some 40 cities and a number of other jurisdictions have passed living wage ordinances. These ordinances mandate that certain businesses, generally those under contract with the city, pay employees a wage high enough to lift their families out of poverty. Indeed, among the cities studied, Neumark finds that living wages have a substantial effect on the wages of workers at the bottom of the scale—and the broader the scope of coverage, the more likely lower-wage workers will be positively affected.

However, as we might expect, he finds a tradeoff between wages and employment. Although living wage laws raise the wages of the urban poor who hold jobs, they also appear to reduce employment levels at the low end of the wage distribution. Once again, targeting subsidy programs is the toughest part of program design. The good news is that Neumark finds that despite individual worker differences, living wages reduce the likelihood that families live in poverty.

One surprising element in this analysis is that Neumark finds sizable wage gains among unionized municipal workers in cities that implement living wage ordinances covering city contractors. He suggests that living wage laws may reduce the incentives for cities to contract out work that would otherwise be done by municipal employees, thus increasing the bargaining power of municipal unions and leading to higher wages. Certainly this would help explain why labor unions—especially those representing municipal workers—are particularly active in the movement to pass living wage ordinances.

It should be noted that although this study finds that living wages may provide some assistance to the urban poor, it does not compare the effectiveness of living wages to other poverty-reduction policies, such as the earned income tax credit, and Neumark observes that policymakers should weigh such alternatives when considering whether to implement a living wage ordinance.

It should also be noted that the summary of this report is written for a lay audience and read alone is sufficient to understand the study's major findings. The body of the report (in particular Chapters 5 through 8) is more technical and is designed to provide the policy specialist and researcher with a detailed description of the methodology and analysis involved in the study. Together they provide an incisive, first-time empirical assessment of the mechanisms and effects of living wage ordinances.

David W. Lyon
President and CEO
Public Policy Institute of California

Summary

Since December 1994, many cities in the United States have passed living wage ordinances. These ordinances typically mandate that businesses under contract with the city, or in some cases receiving assistance from the city (such as subsidies, grants, or tax abatements), must pay their workers a wage sufficient to support a family financially. Baltimore was the first city to pass such legislation, and nearly 40 cities and a number of other jurisdictions have followed suit. Although living wage laws have become popular nationally, California has to some extent been at the forefront of the living wage movement. Four major California cities (Los Angeles, Oakland, San Francisco, and San Jose) have living wage laws on the books, as do six smaller cities (Berkeley, Hayward, Pasadena, San Fernando, Santa Cruz, and West Hollywood). In addition, campaigns to pass living wages are ongoing in other California cities.

The living wage laws in these California cities help to highlight the prominent features of living wage laws nationwide. First, all living wage ordinances feature a minimum wage floor that is higher—and often much higher—than the traditional minimum wages set by state and federal legislation. For example, the current minimum wage in California is $5.75, but living wages range from a low of $7.25 in Pasadena and San Fernando, to $7.69 in Los Angeles, to $9.00 in San Francisco, and to a high of $11.00 in Santa Cruz. Second, living wage laws frequently link the wage floor to a poverty threshold, for example, requiring a wage that would raise a family of four with one full-time worker to the poverty level. Third, coverage by living wage ordinances is far from universal. The most common coverage—and also the most narrow—is restricted to companies under contract with the city. Some living wage laws also impose the wage on companies receiving business assistance from the city. The least common coverage is that imposed by cities on themselves to cover city employees. Regardless, this narrower coverage contrasts with minimum wage laws, which cover nearly all workers. Thus, living wage laws impose high wage floors, have an antipoverty objective that is often reflected in the choice of the wage floor, and often apply to what may constitute a relatively narrow group of workers.

To date, there has been no systematic analysis of the actual effects of living wages on the expected beneficiaries—low-wage workers and lower-income families. Given the fact that a large number of cities have passed living wage laws recently and that campaigns for such laws are under way in many other cities, this is an opportune time to analyze the effects of these laws.

The goal of this monograph is to present such an analysis. Although living wage laws have been adopted in many California cities, the empirical research in this monograph relies on information from living wage laws across the United States, although some attention is given to whether these results also apply to California specifically. The monograph begins by providing some necessary background, in particular (1) describing the evolution of living wage laws in the United States, (2) discussing what economic theory predicts about the effects of living wage laws, and (3) reviewing what we know about the effects of living wage laws from past research on living wages and minimum wages.

The monograph then turns to new research that addresses a broad-ranging set of questions intended to make a significant start on developing a fuller understanding of living wages. In particular, it aims to provide evidence relevant to (1) understanding how living wage laws work and how policy analysts can study their effects, (2) assessing whether living wages achieve their primary policy goal, and (3) understanding the incentives of actors in the economic and political arena to push for living wage laws, and in so doing, asking whether workers other than the intended beneficiaries gain from living wages. Specifically, the following questions are addressed:

- Do living wage laws actually raise wages for at least some low-wage workers? Are living wage laws sufficiently broad and enforced strongly enough to have effects that can be detected in the data available to policy analysts?

- Do living wage laws achieve their stated policy objective of improving economic outcomes for low-wage workers and low-income families? Are wage gains for low-wage workers offset by reductions in employment or in hours worked? Do living wage laws reduce urban poverty?
- Given the stated antipoverty goal of living wage campaigns, why do the laws frequently narrowly restrict coverage to city contractors, rather than imposing wage floors for broad groups of workers? Could one contributing factor be that living wage laws when applied to city contractors reduce the incentives of city governments to privatize, hence strengthening the hand of municipal unions and bringing wage gains to unionized municipal workers, so that there is a potentially powerful constituency for living wage laws that may fall short of the breadth needed to have an effect on poverty?

The goal of the empirical research is to reveal the causal effects of living wage laws. But these (and other) laws are not adopted in a vacuum. Thus, the research strategy must try to sort out causal effects from relationships between outcomes and living wages that arise because of where and when living wage laws are adopted. For example, if living wage laws are adopted where labor markets for low-skill individuals are strong, or where state-level policies encourage work among low-skill individuals, the effects of living wage laws may appear to be more beneficial than they in fact are. As a consequence, the empirical analysis of living wage laws employs a variety of strategies meant to assess whether there are alternative explanations for the relationships found between living wages, on the one hand, and wages, employment, and poverty, on the other. For example, the basic strategy relies on comparing changes in outcomes in cities that did and did not pass living wage laws, to avoid the possibility that living wage laws were adopted in cities in which low-skill individuals on average fare better (or worse). And embellishments of this strategy allow for living wage and non-living wage cities to have different underlying trends in outcomes for low-skill workers, inferring a causal effect only from a break in the trend. Based on the full set of empirical analyses, the following principal findings emerge.

First, there are sizable positive effects of living wage ordinances on the wages of low-wage workers in the cities in which these ordinances are enacted. In particular, the estimates indicate that a 50 percent increase in the living wage (over the minimum wage) would, over the course of a year, raise average wages for workers in the bottom tenth of the wage distribution by 3.5 percent. As an example, for workers otherwise earning the minimum wage in California of $5.75 (in 2000), this represents an average raise of 20 cents per hour. This may appear to be a small increase, but it is an average wage increase experienced by low-wage workers, whereas the actual effect would most likely be a much larger increase concentrated on fewer workers.

In fact, this average increase is larger than would be expected based on the limited coverage of city contractors by the most common type of living wage law. The larger wage effects are generated in cities in which coverage of living wage laws is more broad—specifically, in cities that also impose living wages on employers receiving business assistance from the city—and in these cities the effects of living wage laws are about 50 percent larger than the effects cited above. Thus, existing analyses of the likely effects of living wage laws based on narrow coverage and ignoring business assistance provisions may be quite misleading, and it may be appropriate to think of at least some living wage ordinances—in particular those with business assistance provisions—as operating considerably more broadly than wage floors imposed on city contractors.

Second, although living wage laws raise the wages of low-wage workers, they also appear to reduce employment among the affected workers. In particular, the estimates indicate that a 50 percent increase in the living wage would reduce the employment rate for workers in the bottom tenth of the skill distribution (or equivalently, of the predicted wage distribution) by 7 percent, or 2.8 percentage points. Paralleling the results for wages, the evidence of disemployment effects is stronger for broader business assistance living wage laws. These disemployment effects offset to some extent the positive effects of living wage laws on the wages of low-wage workers, pointing to the tradeoff between wages and employment that economic theory would predict. However, the evidence of disemployment effects is statistically weaker.

Third, although economic theory offers some guidance as to expected tradeoffs between employment and higher mandated wage floors, it makes no predictions regarding the effects of living wage laws on family incomes or poverty. The effects ultimately depend on the family incomes of workers who experience wage gains and those whose employment is reduced. The evidence indicates, however, that the broader business assistance living wage ordinances—which raise wages but at the cost of some disemployment—may moderately reduce urban poverty. The best estimates imply that a 50 percent increase in the living wage would reduce the poverty rate by 1.8 percentage points. Such estimates are not inconsistent with the apparently small wage effects noted above. No one is claiming that living wages lift a family from well below the poverty line to well above it. But living wages may help nudge it over the poverty line. A 20 cent increase in hourly wages translates into $400 of income over the course of the year for a full-time worker. And this is an average effect; the more likely scenario is larger gains concentrated on fewer workers and families. Thus, even coupled with some employment reductions, it is possible that living wages lift a detectable number of families above the poverty line.

Fourth, the evidence points to sizable wage gains for unionized municipal workers when narrow living wage laws covering city contractors are implemented. This evidence is consistent with living wage laws reducing the incentives for cities to contract out work that would otherwise be done by municipal employees, which in turn would be expected to increase the bargaining power of municipal unions and lead to higher wages. As further indirect evidence, labor unions—especially those representing municipal workers—are very active in the movement to pass living wage laws. These findings suggest that a partial explanation of the frequently narrow coverage of living wage laws is that such narrow laws—even if they fail to deliver benefits to low-wage workers or low-income families—benefit unionized municipal workers.

Overall, the combined evidence suggests that the cup is either half full or half empty, depending on one's point of view. Policymakers—whatever their own view of the merits of living wage laws—ought to be encouraged by the finding that living wage laws have their most "direct" intended consequence—raising the wages of low-wage workers.

Economists who put stock in standard economic theory may take some comfort in the finding that wage increases engineered by living wage laws—whatever their other benefits—do lead to some of the predicted tradeoffs in the form of lower employment. Advocates of living wages should be heartened by the results indicating that living wage laws may reduce urban poverty. And finally, those who are skeptical regarding some of the motivations behind unions' support for living wages may find their skepticism reinforced by the evidence that unionized municipal workers reap gains from living wages.

Note, however, that none of these conclusions are necessarily in conflict. Living wage laws can in principle engender some employment losses but, coupled with wage increases and depending on the magnitude and incidence of each of these effects, can also help the poor. And higher-wage unionized municipal workers can gain at the same time that low-income families gain.

A cautious reading of the evidence, then, suggests that, on net, living wages may provide some assistance to the urban poor. This may dispel fears that living wage laws have the unintended effect of increasing urban poverty, but it does not necessarily imply that living wages constitute the best means of helping the urban poor. Policymakers contemplating implementing living wage laws, and policy analysts assessing living wage laws, should give due consideration to comparisons among alternative methods of reducing poverty, such as the Earned Income Tax Credit.

Finally, it is important to emphasize that information on the effects of living wages on low-wage workers and low-income families is only one input—although a crucial one—in providing an overall assessment of living wage policies. Aside from these effects, policymakers should be interested in a number of issues, including the effects of living wages on municipal budgets; on the extent to which higher labor costs are absorbed by contractors or passed through to cities; on taxes, property values, and local economic development; on the provision of city services, stemming from budgetary considerations or the effect of living wages on productivity; on compliance and enforcement; on equity effects (including their effect on women and minorities); and on overall economic welfare. Thus, in and of itself, the evidence presented in this monograph does not lead to a concrete policy recommendation regarding living wages.

However, by finding some evidence that living wages do have a positive effect on wages at the bottom end of the wage distribution and also may lead to modest poverty reductions (despite some employment loss), the monograph suggests that at least some of the claims of living wage advocates are borne out in the data. This suggests that other potential costs and benefits of living wages should be explored to arrive at an overall assessment of the policy, recognizing that the evaluation may well differ depending on the local economy and the specific law considered. Only with a full accounting of the costs and benefits will policymakers, employer organizations, labor unions, and voters be in a position to make informed judgments regarding the merits of this increasingly popular policy innovation.

Acknowledgments

I am grateful to Scott Adams, a Research Fellow in the School of Public Health at the University of Michigan, for collaborating on some of my work on living wages. The material in Chapters 5 through 7 and in some other chapters is based on joint research with him (Neumark and Adams, 2001a and 2001b), and his contribution has been invaluable. Without implying their agreement with my conclusions, I wish to thank the following people for their helpful comments: Eli Berman, Jared Bernstein, Gary Bjork, John DiNardo, Paul Lewis, David Levine, Thomas MaCurdy, Brian Murphy, Rudy Nothenberg, Robert Pollin, Michael Potepan, Deborah Reed, David Reynolds, Steven Rivkin, Peter Schmidt, and seminar participants at the University of California at Berkeley, the University of California at Santa Cruz, Harvard University, the University of Illinois, the University of Missouri, the University of Washington, the Public Policy Institute of California, RAND, and the Federal Reserve Bank of Kansas City. Although all of these people improved the final product, the responsibility for any errors of fact or interpretation is mine. I received some support for this research from the Michigan Applied Public Policy Research Funds at Michigan State University. Most of all, I thank the Public Policy Institute of California for supporting me during my 2000–2001 sabbatical, which allowed my to give my undivided attention to research on living wages.

Contents

Figures

Tables

1. Introduction

Since December 1994, many cities in the United States have passed living wage ordinances. These ordinances typically mandate that businesses under contract with the city, or in some cases receiving assistance from the city, must pay their workers a wage sufficient to support a family financially. Baltimore was the first city to pass such legislation, and nearly 40 cities and a number of other jurisdictions have followed suit. Given the increasing popularity of this policy innovation, an empirical investigation of the effects of living wages is in order, so that we may objectively evaluate the claims of beneficial effects presented by advocates of these ordinances and the claims of adverse effects issued by their opponents.

Descriptions of Living Wage Laws

Although living wage laws have become popular nationally, California has to some extent been at the forefront of their passage. Table 1.1 provides information on living wage laws in large California cities, and Table 1.2 provides information on smaller California cities. Table 1.3 details all remaining city-level living wage laws in the United States. These tables highlight three central features of living wage laws.

First, the feature common to all living wage ordinances is a wage requirement that is higher—and often much higher—than the traditional minimum wages set by state and federal legislation. As shown in Tables 1.1 and 1.2, these wage requirements currently range from $7 or $8 (Los Angeles, Pasadena, and West Hollywood) to near $10 or more (San Jose, Berkeley, and Santa Cruz). These rates are considerably higher than the current minimum wage in California of $5.75. In addition, the required wage is sometimes higher if health insurance is not provided.[1]

---

[1]In the empirical analysis reported in this monograph, the lower wage with health insurance (if there is one) is used, but the qualitative conclusions were not sensitive to using the alternative higher wage.

Table 1.1

Living Wage Laws in Major California Cities

City	Wage Provisions	Coverage Specified in Legislation	External Estimates of Affected Workers and Share of Workforce in Bottom Quartile
Los Angeles	Indexed annually for inflation. Initial wage set to $7.25 with health benefits, $8.50 without: April 1997 ($7.25) June 1998 ($7.37) June 1999 ($7.49) June 2000 ($7.69)	Service contractors > $25,000; assistance > $100,000 or $1 million lump sum	Pollin and Luce (1998): 7,626 (0.81%)
Oakland	Initially set to $8.00 with health benefits, $9.25 without; upwardly adjusted by prior December 31 to December 31 change in the Bay Area Consumer Price Index: April 1998 ($8.00) April 1999 ($8.15) April 2000 ($8.35)	Contractors > $25,000; assistance > $100,000	
San Francisco	August 2000 ($9.00), plus $1.25 per hour for health insurance, rising to $10.00 in 12–18 months	Service contractors > $25,000 ($50,000 for nonprofits); airport leaseholders; home health care workers	Reich et al. (1999): 4,800 (2.14%); Alunan et al. (1999): 4,766 (1.97%)
San Jose	$9.50 with health benefits, $10.75 without; reset each February to the new poverty level for a family of three and adjusted upward for higher San Jose cost of living— approximately a 45% premium: December 1998 ($9.50) March 1999 ($9.68) March 2000 ($9.92)	Service contractors > $20,000; assistance > $100,000 (excludes trainees and workers under age 18); city employees	Williams (1998): 600 (0.37%)

Table 1.2

Living Wage Laws, Smaller California Cities

City	Wage Provisions	Coverage Specified in Legislation
Berkeley	June 2000 ($9.75)	Companies conducting business with the city and lessees
Hayward	April 1999 ($8.00 with health benefits, $9.25 without; adjusted annually on April 1 for cost of living in Bay Area)	City employees; contractors and subcontractors > $25,000— maintenance, custodial, landscaping, laundry, temporary, pest, security, and social services
Pasadena	September 1998 ($7.25 with health benefits, $8.50 without)	Contractors > $25,000; city employees
Santa Cruz	October 2000 ($11.00 with health benefits, $12.00 without)	City employees and contractors
San Fernando	April 2000 ($7.25 with health benefits, $8.50 without)	Contractors > $25,000
West Hollywood	October 1997 (initially, $7.25 with health benefits, $8.50 without; adjusted annually as the City Employees Retirement System benefits are adjusted)	Service contractors > $25,000 and entering into a contract of at least three months

NOTE: This table includes only cities for which the data yield a sufficient number of observations to obtain reliable estimates.

Table 1.4 compares the levels of living wages with minimum wages and the wages of relatively low-wage workers, highlighting the wide gaps in most cities between legislated living wages and minimum wages and sometimes also between living wages and wages at the low end of the labor market. All the living wages except Buffalo's exceeded the federal minimum wage ($5.15) by at least 30 percent in 2000, and the median living wage ($8.19) was 59 percent higher. In Hartford and San Jose, living wages exceeded the federal minimum by at least 82 percent and exceeded the higher state minimum wages effective in these cities by more than 52 percent. Looking above the minimum wage, the living

Table 1.3

Living Wage Laws in Cities in Other States

City	Wage Provisions	Coverage Specified in Legislation	External Estimates of Affected Workers and Share of Workforce in Bottom Quartile
Baltimore	December 1994; wage requirements were as follows: July 1995 ($6.10) July 1996 ($6.60) July 1997 ($7.10) July 1998 ($7.70) July 1999 ($7.90)	Contractors > $5,000	Niedt et al. (1999): 1,494–5,976 (0.51–2.05%)
Boston	September 1998 (100% of poverty level)	Contractors > $100,000; subcontractors > $25,000 (> 25 employees)	
Buffalo	July 1999; wage requirement of $6.22 starting in 2000	Contractors and subcontractors > $50,000 (> 10 employees)	
Cambridge	September 1998 ($8.23)	City employees, contractors, and subcontractors > $10,000; recipients of business assistance > $10,000	
Chicago	July 1998 ($7.60)	Contractors and subcontractors > 25 employees	Tolley et al. (1999): 9,807 (1.01%)
Corvallis (OR)	November 1999 ($9.00)	Contractors > $5,000	
Dayton	April 1998 ($7.00)	City employees	
Denver	March 2000 (100% of poverty level; assumes 2,080 annual hours)	Contractors and subcontractors > $2,000	

4

Table 1.3 (continued)

City	Wage Provisions	Coverage Specified in Legislation	External Estimates of Affected Workers and Share of Workforce in Bottom Quartile
Detroit	November 1998 (100% of poverty level with health benefits, 125% without)	Contractors, subcontractors, and financial assistance recipients > $50,000	Reynolds (1999): 2,300 (0.40%)
Duluth	July 1997 ($6.50 with health benefits, $7.25 without)	Recipients of grants, low interest loans, or direct aid > $25,000; 10% of employees exempted	
Durham	January 1998 ($7.55)	Contractors and city employees	
Hartford	October 1999 (110% of poverty level)	Contractors > $50,000; commercial development projects receiving subsidies > $100,000	
Jersey City	June 1996 ($7.50 with health benefits)	Contractors	
Madison	March 1999 (100% of poverty level for family of four in 1999, 105% in 2000, 110% in 2001)	Contractors and subcontractors > $5,000; assistance > $100,000; nonunion city employees	
Milwaukee	November 1995 (set to poverty level for family of three on March 1 of each year; assumes 2,080 annual hours)	Contractors and subcontractors > $5,000	
Minneapolis	March 1997 (100% of poverty level for family of four with health benefits, 110% without)	Assistance > $100,000 initially, > $25,000 as of December 1998	
New Haven	April 1997 (initially 100% of poverty level for a family of four, 120% of poverty level phased in over 5 years)	Contractors	
Omaha	May 2000 ($8.19 with health benefits, $9.01 without)	City employees, contractors > $75,000, assistance > $75,000	

Table 1.3 (continued)

City	Wage Provisions	Coverage Specified in Legislation	External Estimates of Affected Workers and Share of Workforce in Bottom Quartile
Portland	July 1996 ($7.00) July 1998 ($7.50) July 1999 ($8.00)	Custodial, security, and parking attendant contracts	
St. Louis	August 2000 (130% of poverty level for a family of three; assumes 2,080 annual hours)	Contractors and businesses receiving tax breaks	
St. Paul	September 1998 (100% of poverty level for family of four with health benefits, 110% without)	Recipients of assistance > $100,000	
San Antonio	July 1998 ($9.27 to 70% of service employees in new jobs; $10.13 to 70% of durable goods workers)	Businesses receiving tax breaks	
Somerville (MA)	May 1999 ($8.35 with health benefits)	City employees, contractors, and subcontractors	
Tucson	September 1999 ($8.00 with health benefits, $9.00 without)	Contractors; recipients of economic development assistance > $100,000 annually	
Warren (MI)	January 2000 (100% of poverty level for family of four with health benefits, 125% without)	Contractors; businesses receiving subsidies > $50,000	
Ypsilanti (MI)	May 1999 ($8.50 with health benefits, $10.00 without)	Contractors > $5,000 (> 10 employees); nonprofits receiving > $10,000 in assistance	

SOURCES: Much of the information for this table was obtained through correspondence with city governments. Some data, however, were obtained through information made publicly available by the Employment Policies Institute (www.epionline.org) and the Association of Community Organizations for Reform Now (www.acorn.org).

NOTES: Some cities are listed in some sources as having living wage ordinances but instead have prevailing wage laws covering construction (e.g., New York, Gary, and Memphis). Other cities, such as Des Moines, have an average wage goal policy rather than a living wage law. In addition to the cities in the table, one school district and numerous counties that have adopted living wage ordinances are listed by the Employment Policies Institute.

Table 1.4

Living Wages, Minimum Wages, and 10th Centiles of Wage Distribution in Selected U.S. Cities, 2000

	Living Wage	Minimum Wage	10th Centile
All living wage cities, overall	—	—	6.67
Baltimore	7.90	5.15	6.92
Boston	8.53	6.00	8.00
Buffalo	6.22	5.15	6.00
Chicago	7.60	5.15	6.73
Dayton	7.00	5.15	6.25
Denver	8.20	5.15	7.50
Detroit	8.53	5.15	7.00
Durham	7.55	5.15	7.50
Hartford	9.38	6.15	7.75
Jersey City	7.50	5.15	6.25
Los Angeles	7.69	5.75	5.75
Milwaukee	6.80	5.15	7.25
Minneapolis	8.53	5.15	8.00
Oakland	8.35	5.75	8.00
Omaha	8.19	5.15	7.00
Portland	8.00	6.50	7.00
St. Louis	8.84	5.15	6.50
San Antonio	9.27	5.15	6.00
San Francisco	9.00	5.75	7.50
San Jose	9.92	5.75	8.00
Tucson	8.00	5.15	6.00

NOTES: Tenth centile estimates are weighted and computed over all months of 2000. The latest living wages and minimum wages in 2000 are shown, using the lower living wage (with health insurance). This table includes only cities for which the data yield a sufficient number of observations to obtain reliable estimates.

wage exceeded the 10th centile in nearly every city, although the 10th centile wage was within $1 of the living wage in over half of them.[2]

---

[2]Although city employees are generally not covered by living wages, it is possible to compare their wages with living wages for the few cities where they are covered and where there are sufficient numbers of observations. In particular, we can compare living wages with wages for state and local government workers—some of whom are covered by living wage laws—in Durham, Dayton, and San Jose. Here, it seems sensible to do the comparison only with non-living wage cities because the wages of more low-wage state and local government workers in cities with living wages are likely to be directly affected. Among these cities, the government worker at the 10th centile earned an hourly wage of $8.00 in the South, $8.08 in the Midwest, and $8.65 in the West. Thus, for two of the three cities (Dayton and San Jose), the living wage exceeds the comparison wage at the 10th centile for state and local government workers.

A second feature of living wage laws is that the wage requirements are typically linked to definitions of family poverty. Many ordinances explicitly peg the living wage to the level needed for a family to reach the federal poverty line (e.g., San Jose, Milwaukee, and St. Paul). Thus, when the federal government defines new poverty levels each year, the living wages in these cities increase. Other localities set an initial wage that is increased annually to take into account increases in the cost of living (e.g., Los Angeles and Oakland). Although these latter ordinances may not explicitly state the basis for setting the initial wage, poverty is undoubtedly an underlying factor.

Third, coverage by living wage ordinances is far from universal. Some cities impose wage floors only on companies under contract with the city (generally including nonprofits) (e.g., West Hollywood, Milwaukee, and Boston); this is the most common specification of coverage. Others also impose the wage on companies receiving business assistance from the city (e.g., Los Angeles and Oakland); in almost every case, this is in addition to coverage of city contractors. A few cities also impose the requirement on themselves and pay city employees a living wage (e.g., San Jose and Pasadena). Of the 36 city living wage laws listed in Tables 1.1 through 1.3, which provide a current comprehensive list,[3] 31 cover contractors, 14 cover employers receiving some form of business assistance, and 10 cover city employees.[4] Thus, contractor coverage is by far the most common feature, and coverage of city employees is the least common.

The living wage laws covering employers receiving business assistance, which figure prominently in some of the ensuing analysis, are sometimes vague and somewhat heterogeneous. For some cities, the provision is relatively general. For example, the ordinance in Minneapolis refers to employers receiving economic development assistance, whereas in Los Angeles and Oakland the ordinances refer to financial assistance generally, which could presumably entail grants, tax

---

[3]The Employment Policies Institute maintains a comprehensive listing of current living wage laws and ongoing living wage campaigns on its web page (www.epionline. org).

[4]Among the larger cities on which this monograph focuses, living wage laws covering city employees are even more rare.

abatements, etc.[5] For others, more specific criteria are provided. For example, San Antonio's living wage law covers businesses receiving tax breaks, and Hartford's covers commercial development projects receiving more than $100,000 in city subsidies or financing.

It is very difficult to estimate how many workers are covered and hence are potentially directly affected by living wage laws. For a few cities, researchers have made estimates of the number of workers likely to be directly affected by living wage laws, according to both coverage and whether the worker's wage was below the proposed living wage. Those making these estimates have used a variety of sources and methods, including direct information on city contracts, "back-of-the-envelope" calculations, and surveys of employers. Some of these estimates are summarized in the last columns of Tables 1.1 and 1.3. The numbers of affected workers listed are taken directly from the cited reports. To get a better idea of the "bite" of these laws, those tables also report the share of the workforce in the lower quartile of the wage distribution in each city represented by the number of covered workers. Using the lowest quartile is appropriate because among the cities with a living wage effective in a particular month, the living wage was below the 25th percentile in 82 percent of cases. For the most part, these estimated shares are very low— in the 1 percent range. However, these estimates focus on the coverage of employees of city contractors, not on the potentially broader coverage that also extends to employers receiving business assistance from the city. They also generally ignore "spillover" effects on other low-wage workers not directly covered by the laws, but who might nonetheless see wage increases, and higher-wage workers whose wages might increase in response to a living wage. In that sense, then, these estimates probably should be viewed as lower bounds for the numbers and shares of affected workers.

---

[5]Although these general provisions do not always spell out what is meant by "financial assistance," some city ordinances provide detailed rules and regulations. For example, Oakland's rules and regulations specify that this includes (but is not limited to) grants, rent subsidies, bond financing, loans below market rates, financial planning, tax increment financing, land writedowns, provision of on-site improvements, tax credits and rebates, loan guarantees, and sale of city property for less than fair market value.

These features of living wage laws may counter two common perceptions regarding these laws. First, living wages typically do not cover city employees. Second, although existing coverage estimates are very low, this may be because they tend to ignore coverage of employers receiving business assistance—coverage that is specified in a number of living wage laws.

Of course, living wage laws (like any laws) require enforcement and penalties if they are to have an effect. Some city laws are relatively vague concerning enforcement but some are quite explicit. Table 1.5 provides details about living wage laws in major California cities. Oakland's law is most explicit regarding enforcement procedures, including a description of an office of contract compliance to review payroll reports, fringe benefits, time cards, etc.[6] It is common in California cities and other cities to allow employees to initiate complaints, while barring retaliation by employers. Most laws specify that violators can be barred from future city contracts for some period of time, and many also specify financial penalties. Finally, it is common to allow recourse to the courts. However, as yet no hard data exist on enforcement activity, such as violations reported and penalties imposed.

Research Goals and Questions

To date, there has been no systematic empirical evaluation of the actual effects of living wages on the expected beneficiaries—low-wage workers and their families. Because an increasing number of cities have passed living wage laws recently and campaigns for such legislation are under way in many other cities, it is critical to analyze the effects of these laws on low-wage workers and poor families.

The goal of this monograph is to present such an evaluation. Relatively few California cities have adopted living wage laws. Thus, empirical research must rely on information from living wage laws in other states as well, although some attention is given to whether these results also apply to California specifically. The monograph addresses three broad-ranging sets of questions, which are intended to provide

---

[6]Sander and Lokey (1998) describe compliance and enforcement efforts in Los Angeles.

Table 1.5

Living Wage Enforcement, Major California Cities

Los Angeles

Enforcement (Section 10-37-5)
Employee claiming violation may bring action in Municipal Court or Superior Court.

May be awarded back pay for the period of violation, for failure to pay minimum wages; the difference in the required wage with and without benefits for the period of violation, for failure to pay medical benefits; attorney's fees.

Oakland

Penalties for noncompliance (Regulation 10)
Noncompliance may result in a penalty of $500 per week or exclusion from bidding on or participating in future contracts for one year.

Monitoring and investigation (Regulation 11)
Office of contract compliance will review payroll reports, fringe benefit statements, and time cards; after notification, continued noncompliance will result in the office issuing a notice to withhold compensation owed under the contract.

Employee complaint process (Regulation 12)
Employees may report violations to the city, with identity revealed only with worker's consent; retaliation by the employer is prohibited.

Enforcement (Regulation 13)
Remedies include suspension or termination of the contract or financial assistance agreement; requirement that the employer pay back any or all of the amount disbursed by the city; deeming the employer ineligible for future city contracts or financial assistance until penalties and restitution are paid in full; imposition of a fine payable to the city of $500 for each week for each employee not paid in accordance with law; wage restitution for each employee.

Table 1.5 (continued)

San Jose

Enforcement (Section IV.D)

City may suspend or terminate the contract; require the employer to pay any amounts underpaid in violation of the required payments, the city's administrative costs, and in the case of financial assistance any sums disbursed by the city; bar the contractor from future city contracts or deem the recipient ineligible for future financial assistance.

San Francisco

Administration and enforcement (Section 12P.6)

A covered employee may report any violation to the Department of Administrative Services; the agency will keep the employee's identify confidential, to the extent allowed by law.

If the contractor fails to comply, the agency can charge the contractor an amount equal to the difference between the minimum compensation levels required by the law and actual compensation, plus interest, and the right to set this off against amounts due to the contractor; terminate the contract in whole or in part; seek reinstatement and other relief for any action taken by the contractor in retaliation against an employee; bar a contractor from future contracts for three years.

Covered employees can bring action in Superior Court, seeking back pay and reinstatement or relief for any act of retaliation.

evidence relevant to (1) understanding how living wage laws work and how policy analysts can study their effects, (2) assessing whether living wages achieve their primary policy goal, and (3) understanding the incentives of actors in the economic and political arena to push for living wage laws. These questions are as follows:

- Do living wage laws have any "teeth," raising wages for at least some low-wage workers? Are living wage laws sufficiently broad and enforced strongly enough to have effects that can be detected in the data available to policy analysts?
- Do living wage laws achieve their stated policy objective of improving economic outcomes for low-wage workers and low-income families? Are wage gains for low-wage workers offset by reductions in employment or in hours worked? Do living wage laws reduce urban poverty?
- Given the stated antipoverty goal of living wage campaigns, why do the laws frequently narrowly restrict coverage to city contractors, rather than imposing wage floors for broad groups of workers? Is one of the contributing factors that living wage laws applied to city contractors reduce the incentives of city governments to privatize, hence strengthening the hand of municipal unions and bringing wage gains to unionized municipal workers, so that there is a potentially powerful constituency for living wage laws that may fall short of the breadth needed to have an effect on poverty?

Overview of This Report

Chapters 2 through 4 lay the groundwork for evaluating living wage effects. Chapter 2 discusses the effects of living wage laws predicted by standard economic models and by some of the unique features of living wage laws. Chapter 3 presents findings from research on *minimum* wages that may be informative about the effects of living wages and provides a roadmap for how to evaluate the effects of living wages. Chapter 4 summarizes and critiques existing research on living wages and clarifies the contributions of this monograph.

The next four chapters present the original research used to evaluate living wages. Chapter 5 estimates the effects of living wage laws on the wages of workers who are supposed to be the beneficiaries of these laws and discusses many of the research issues involved in evaluating living wage ordinances. Chapter 6 examines the employment effects of living wages, and Chapter 7 focuses primarily on whether living wages reduce urban poverty. Chapter 8 addresses some of the factors that shape living wage laws, in particular asking whether the frequent restrictions of coverage to city contractors can be explained at least in part as attempts by municipal unions to insulate their workers against competition from private contractors. Finally, Chapter 9 summarizes the monograph, considers the implications of the findings, and discusses questions that remain to be answered in future research on living wage laws.

2. Theoretical Predictions of the Effects of Living Wages

Although city living wage ordinances have received little attention from academic researchers, the effects of standard federal or state minimum wages have been studied extensively, both theoretically and empirically. However, there are important reasons why the effects of living wage ordinances may be quite different from those of minimum wages. As a result, original research on living wage ordinances is needed to draw reliable conclusions. The existing work on standard minimum wages provides a useful road map for analyzing the consequences of living wage ordinances. This chapter reviews what economic theory tells us about the potential effects of minimum wage floors, with some discussion of the unique features of living wage laws.

Predicted Effects of Living Wages for Low-Wage Workers

Living wage ordinances are binding for some covered employers, forcing them to raise wages of some workers. However, identifying these employers and the number of workers likely to be bound by the minimum wage requirement, and also the extent to which their current wages fall short of the required wage, is likely to prove a difficult task.[1] Nonetheless, proceeding from the point of view that at least some employers will face higher costs for some workers, standard economic analysis makes some predictions regarding the effects of these ordinances.

Employers in both the for-profit and nonprofit sectors are assumed to minimize the costs of production, which depend in perhaps complex ways on the relative prices of the different inputs used to produce their

---

[1]For an ambitious effort in the context of a proposed living wage ordinance in San Francisco, see Alunan et al. (1999).

particular good or service, as well as the production technology. Although relatively little is known about the specific constraints and choices facing an employer, economic theory predicts that a government-mandated increase in the price of one input—in this case low-skilled labor—leads to two sets of effects. The first occurs as employers substitute away from the now more expensive input and toward other inputs. For example, depending on the good or service under consideration, employers may hire fewer low-skilled workers (or, more precisely, use fewer low-skilled labor hours) and employ more high-skilled labor. Alternatively, they may mechanize some tasks previously performed by low-skilled labor, substituting toward capital. Even if it is not possible to predict precisely the way employers will substitute, they will certainly use less low-skilled labor.

The second set of effects occurs because this substitution away from low-skilled labor and toward other inputs raises the costs of production, resulting in higher prices to customers and less overall output (or smaller scale). This follows from the assumption that employers are minimizing costs in the first place, which implies that imposition of a minimum wage requirement can only result in higher cost. When costs rise, though, the price charged for the good or service will rise. In a private market, this will reduce demand for the product and, hence, lower the use of all of its variable inputs. These scale effects differ from substitution effects in that they entail an overall scaling back of the employer's outputs and inputs, whereas substitution effects concern changing the mix of inputs. However, *both* effects reduce the employment of low-skilled labor.[2] Nonetheless, at least four unique features are likely to weaken the effects of living wages relative to the effects of standard minimum wages.

First, cities purchase goods and services from contractors and possibly also from grantees. Thus, the quantity of goods or services demanded may not fall with price increases (or the demand curve may not slope downward), or at least not appreciably over some range, either because the city is able to raise taxes to cover higher costs (thus largely

---

[2] In contrast, substitution and scale effects may have opposite effects on the use of other inputs such as high-skilled labor.

allowing contractors to pass through the increased labor costs), or because some services have to be purchased in quantities that may be largely insensitive to price (such as snow plowing). However, some factors work to counter this moderation of disemployment effects. A city government surely has some limits on its ability to raise taxes. In addition, living wage ordinances may raise wages for work other than that done in fulfillment of city contracts. For example, city contractors or recipients of assistance may pay higher wages to workers who are producing goods and services sold on the private market as well— perhaps the same workers who do some covered work and some uncovered work, or different workers working for the same employer.[3] The responses to wage increases for work done in the private sector are more likely to be subject to downward-sloping demand.

Second, because living wage laws specify wage levels that must be paid without reference to the skill levels of workers, to comply, employers who do some work covered by these laws and some work that is not covered may reallocate their higher-skilled and higher-wage labor to the former and their lower-skilled and lower-wage labor to the latter. This may still entail some inefficiencies but could moderate any cost-increasing effects.

Third, even under broad definitions of coverage by living wage ordinances, only a fraction of the workforce is likely to be covered, in contrast to the near-universal coverage of minimum wage laws. The effects of a wage floor with a covered and an uncovered sector have been modeled by Mincer (1976). In such a situation, some of the labor disemployed in the covered sector is likely to shift into the uncovered sector. This has two consequences. First, because wages in that sector

---

[3]The pass-through of higher mandated wages for low-wage workers to high-wage workers in the same firm is labeled "ripple effects" in the minimum wage literature. Alunan et al. (1999) distinguish between "vertical" ripple effects, which may arise when employers raise the wages of those initially above the living wage to preserve wage differentials between workers, and "horizontal" ripple effects, which may arise when employers raise the wages of workers who may not be covered by a living wage law (e.g., they do not work on city contracts) to preserve parity with other workers at the firm who are covered. Generally speaking, employees of covered firms who do not work on contracts are not explicitly covered by living wage laws, although Detroit's law extends to all workers at covered work sites.

can adjust downward in response to the outward supply shift, wages may fall for *all* low-skilled workers in that sector.[4] Second, this results in lower costs of production, leading to lower output prices and higher employment and output. However, employment will not expand enough in the uncovered sector to offset fully the employment decline in the covered sector.[5]

Mincer's model was developed to analyze minimum wages, but two potentially important differences exist between minimum wage laws and living wage ordinances. First, as a purely quantitative matter, even under broad definitions of coverage by living wage ordinances, the uncovered sector is likely to be large. As a consequence, it seems relatively unlikely that there would be a substantial lowering of low-skilled workers' wages in the uncovered private sector, although this may occur in a subset of industries or occupations in which workers disemployed from the covered sector happen to be highly concentrated. Second, one substantive difference from the traditional model is that the sector of the economy not covered by the living wage ordinance nonetheless is covered by the minimum wage. This introduces a wage floor in the uncovered sector, which may restrict the ability of wages to fall. If this wage floor becomes binding, it will restrict the extent to which employment can expand in the uncovered sector, exacerbating the overall disemployment effects of the ordinance and moderating any wage declines. The predicted effects of living wages on low-wage workers in the covered and uncovered sectors, and the predicted net effects, are summarized in Table 2.1.

---

[4]An exception is when workers leave the uncovered sector to "queue" for covered-sector jobs in sufficient numbers (Mincer, 1976). However, this requires—among other conditions—that work in the uncovered sector deters search for higher-paying jobs in the covered sector.

[5]Formally, this results because when the supply of labor shifts out in the uncovered sector, the decline in wages leads some workers to choose nonemployment (or reduced hours). Whether these displaced workers are *unemployed* depends on whether they continue to seek work, as the definition of unemployment includes both being available for work *and* looking for work. Because the decision to look for work may depend on a variety of factors, analyses of minimum wages—and the analysis of the living wage ordinances in this monograph—focus on employment versus nonemployment, rather than unemployment.

Table 2.1

Predicted Effects of Living Wages on Wages and Employment of Low-Wage Workers in the Covered Sector, the Uncovered Sector, and Overall

	Covered Workers	Uncovered Workers	Predicted Net Effect	Reason for Predicted Net Effect
Wages effect	Positive	Negative	Positive	Minimum wage floor constrains wage declines in uncovered sector
Employment effect	Negative	Positive	Negative	Wage decline in uncovered sector leads to lower labor force participation

Fourth, the scale effect ultimately stems from cost increases caused by the substitution induced by the living wage. The conclusion that costs must increase is based on the assumption that employers minimize costs in the first place. However, it is conceivable that government contracting is done in an uncompetitive environment in which pressures to minimize costs are mitigated, in which case employers may find ways to offset the increased labor costs for low-wage labor by reducing costs in other dimensions. This idea has its origins in the X-inefficiency theory of Leibenstein (1978).[6]

There are many reasons, therefore, to expect disemployment effects from living wage laws to be moderated—in particular relative to effects of a general wage floor imposed on the private sector. Nonetheless, economic theory predicts that these disemployment effects will occur. And one final factor that may lead to stronger disemployment effects is the significantly higher wage floor typically imposed by living wage laws. Overall, then, the effects of living wage laws on employers are likely to entail reduced employment of low-skilled labor, as well as lower output, higher output prices, and ambiguous changes in the use of other inputs—although increased use of at least some of these other inputs is more likely if scale effects are dominated by substitution effects.

---

[6]For evidence on efficiency in the private and public sectors, see, for example, Bhattacharyya and Parker (1994), Hollas and Stansell (1994), and Kuo-Ping and Kao (1992).

Thus, among the low-skilled workers who are the intended beneficiaries of living wage ordinances, there are likely to be winners and losers. The biggest winners are those whose wages are forced up and who retain their jobs (and hours) with covered employers. The biggest losers are those who lose their jobs with covered employers and end up working at lower-wage jobs in the uncovered sector or perhaps nonemployed. There are some additional possible winners and losers. First, as low-skilled workers disemployed from the covered sector shift to the uncovered sector, wages there may be bid down somewhat. Second, high-skilled workers could gain or lose, depending on the relative strength of substitution and scale effects. Finally, there may be wage increases for higher-skilled workers attributable to the ripple effects described above, if employers raise the wages of workers above the mandated wage floor to maintain relative wage differentials, although such wage increases can also occur as a response to increased demand for higher-skilled workers (Gramlich, 1976; Grossman, 1983).

Other Effects of Living Wage Laws

The responses considered thus far are "first-round" effects focusing on the labor market. However, there may be "second-round" effects as employers react to living wage laws. Although these second-round effects are not the focus of this monograph, they raise potentially important caution flags for policymakers and suggest questions for future research; they thus bear some discussion.

Unlike an increase in the national (or a state) minimum wage, which covers nearly all employers and leaves them essentially no choice but to pay the higher wage, employers affected by living wage ordinances may in some cases find it more profitable to terminate contracts, grants, abatements, etc., with the city. This is more likely to occur, of course, when the costs imposed by the minimum wage requirement are too great to pass through to cities. In particular, firms are more likely to take this step the greater their reliance on low-skilled labor, all else the same.

These "second-round" responses have some potentially negative implications. First, firms most likely to "select out" of city business are those employing the highest shares of low-wage workers—precisely the workers whom these ordinances are intended to help in the first place.

Second, as some firms terminate their city contracts, fewer firms are left to bid on city contracts, which may—if the number of remaining firms becomes sufficiently small—lead to less competitive bidding and therefore higher prices for city services. On the other hand, the decision of some employers to select out of city contracts and grants may increase private-sector competition and lower prices there. Finally, living wage laws may have an additional adverse consequence if some of the affected recipients of business assistance that subsequently withdraw or reduce services are nonprofit organizations catering to needy individuals and families.

Living Wages and Low-Income Families

This chapter has thus far discussed in some detail how living wage laws may affect low-wage workers. However, as noted in Chapter 1, the goal of living wages is not necessarily to help low-wage workers but rather to help low-income families. The distinction is important because low-wage workers are far from synonymous with low-income families. Although there are few poor or low-income families with high-wage workers, there are many high-income families with low-wage workers (such as teenagers). This point has been made quite forcefully in the minimum wage literature. For example, considering the 1990 increase in the federal minimum wage, Burkhauser et al. (1996) estimated that although one-third of workers likely to be affected by this increase were in poor or near-poor families (defined as those with family incomes up to 1.5 times the poverty line based on their family's size), roughly another one-third were in families with incomes exceeding three times the poverty line.[7]

Thus, when the wage paid to low-wage workers is forced up by law, the consequences for low-income families depend on where the "winners" and "losers" among low-wage workers are in the family income distribution. For example, if the job loss from a living wage is concentrated among low-wage workers in relatively affluent families (most likely teenagers), whereas the wage gains are concentrated among

---

[7] O'Brien-Strain and MaCurdy (2000) show that the same argument applies to the distributional effects of minimum wages in California.

low-wage single-parent heads of household, it is considerably more likely that a living wage would help poor or low-income families. The opposite scenario is also possible, with the job loss concentrated among low-wage workers in low-income families, in which case poor families could be hurt by living wage laws.

This potentially poor "targeting" of living wage laws is also reflected in the way these laws are written. As documented in Chapter 1, living wage ordinances are not flexible regarding family size, even though poverty levels vary dramatically depending on the number of children and adults in a household. As an example, consider a city that sets its wage floor to the federal poverty threshold for a family of four with two children, which was $16,530 in 1998. This implies an hourly wage of $8.27 for a typical worker who logs 2,000 hours in a year. The poverty level for a single adult, however, is only $8,480. The ordinances do not allow employers to pay single adults a lower wage.[8] Similarly, the ordinances do not take account of the income of other family members, who could conceivably be earning high incomes. As a simple example, if two adults are working for a covered contractor or grantee, both would receive the living wage, placing their incomes well above the poverty level.

Ultimately, assessing the effects of living wage laws on low-income families is a purely empirical question. Economic theory predicts that some low-wage workers will gain and others will lose, but it is uninformative about the incidence of these gains and losses with respect to family income.

---

[8]Of course, a higher minimum wage for workers from needier families would not be desirable, as this would reduce the relative demand for these workers. This point emphasizes the potential advantages of income-support policies based on family income (rather than individual income or wages), such as the Earned Income Tax Credit (EITC) (see, e.g., Neumark and Wascher, 2001).

3. Lessons from Research on Minimum Wages

Living wage laws differ from minimum wage laws for numerous reasons—including higher wage floors, more narrow coverage, and application to the public sector. Nonetheless, there is an extensive literature on minimum wages, which, by providing a legally mandated wage floor, have an obvious parallel to living wages. Consequently, this chapter briefly reviews the available evidence on the effects of minimum wages to learn more about their potential effects on low-wage workers and on low-income and poor families. Clearly, though, living wage laws require independent empirical evaluation.

The Employment Effects of Minimum Wages

Labor economists have written many papers testing the prediction that minimum wages reduce the employment of low-skilled workers. Earlier studies used aggregate time-series data for the United States to estimate the effects of changes in the national minimum wage.[1] The consensus from these first-generation studies was that the elasticity of employment of low-skilled (young) workers with respect to minimum wages was most likely between −0.1 and −0.2 (Brown et al., 1982); that is, for every 10 percent increase in the minimum wage, employment of these low-skilled individuals falls by 1 to 2 percent.

More recent studies have used panel data covering multiple states over a period of years to study the effects of changes in minimum wages at the state level. This approach permits researchers to abstract from aggregate economic changes that may be correlated with minimum wages. Such correlation can make it difficult to untangle the effects of minimum wages in aggregate time-series data (e.g., Neumark and

---

[1]Brown et al. (1983) is a good example of such a study.

Wascher, 1992; Card and Krueger, 1994). Evidence from these second-generation studies has spurred considerable controversy regarding whether or not minimum wages reduce the employment of low-skilled workers, with some labor economists arguing that the new evidence shows that the predictions of the standard model are wrong and that minimum wages fail to reduce and may even increase employment (Card and Krueger, 1995).

On the other hand, much recent evidence using similar sorts of data tends to confirm the prediction that minimum wages reduce the employment of low-skilled workers. The estimated effects often parallel the earlier time-series evidence indicating that the elasticity of employment of low-skilled workers with respect to the minimum wage is in the -0.1 to -0.2 range, with estimates for teenagers—who have often been the focus of minimum wage research—closer to -0.1 (Burkhauser et al., 2000; Neumark and Wascher, 1996, 2000; Zavodny, 2000). As further evidence, a leading economics journal recently published a survey including economists' views of the best estimates of minimum wage effects. Results of this survey, which was conducted in 1996—after most of the recent research on minimum wages was well-known to economists—indicated that the median "best estimate" of the minimum wage elasticity for teenagers was -0.1, whereas the mean estimate was -0.21 (Fuchs et al., 1998). Thus, although there may be some outlying perspectives, economists' views of the effects of the minimum wage are centered in the range of the earlier estimates and many of the more recent estimates of the disemployment effects of minimum wages.

Minimum Wages and Low-Wage Workers

In asking whether minimum wages raise the incomes of low-wage workers, it is often assumed that an elasticity as small as -0.1 or -0.2 implies only minor disemployment effects and hence is sound public policy. However, the argument that "small" estimated minimum wage effects imply that minimum wages raise the incomes of low-wage workers is flawed. One problem with using a -0.1 or -0.2 elasticity to make this argument is that such estimates are taken from studies of the employment effects of minimum wages for entire age groups and are not equivalent to—as some have asserted—the elasticity of demand for minimum wage workers. An estimate of the effect of a minimum wage increase on total employment in any particular age group is really the effect on the low-wage individuals in the group for whom the new minimum wage raises wages, averaged over all workers in this age category. Because high-wage workers are, for the most part, unaffected by changes in the minimum wage, the aggregate elasticity will likely understate the employment effect on the affected workers.[2]

In addition, the conventional elasticity uses the legislated minimum wage increase as the denominator, whereas the wage increases received by workers below the new minimum are typically smaller, since many of these workers earn wages above the old minimum initially. Reducing the denominator in the elasticity also increases its absolute magnitude. Finally, the focus on employment effects ignores the effects on hours worked, which could be more widespread than disemployment effects but equally damaging to earnings.

One consideration acting in the opposite direction, however, is that there may be wage increases for workers a bit above the minimum wage, as discussed above. Such effects are potentially quite important in assessing the consequences of minimum wages for low-wage workers (and low-income families) in the United States. Because of the relatively low level of the minimum wage historically in this country, many workers earning above the minimum would nonetheless be considered low-wage workers, and a sizable proportion of them are in poor and near-poor families.

Recent research has considered the effects of minimum wages on employment, hours worked, wages, and ultimately the labor income of workers at different points in the wage distribution (Neumark et al., 1999). This research indicates that workers initially earning near the minimum wage are, on net, adversely affected by minimum wage increases, but, not surprisingly, higher-wage workers are little affected. Although the wages of low-wage workers increase, their hours of work and employment decline, and the combined effect of these changes is a decline in earned income.

---

[2]See Neumark and Wascher (forthcoming) for a thorough discussion of this point.

Minimum Wages and Low-Income Families

As noted in Chapter 2, although there are few poor or low-income families with high-wage workers, there are many high-income families with low-wage workers (Burkhauser et al., 1996). Theoretical economic analysis offers no predictions as to whether minimum wages will benefit poor or low-income families; this is purely an empirical question. Recent research indicates that past experience with minimum wage increases in the United States is at odds with the claim that raising the minimum will help lift families out of poverty. Rather, raising the minimum wage does not reduce the proportion of families living in poverty and, if anything, increases it, thus *raising* the poverty rate (Golan et al., 2001; Neumark et al., 1998).[3]

Summary

In summary, the evidence indicates that increases in wage floors acting through the minimum wage fail to accomplish their principal policy goal of raising the incomes of low-wage workers or of poor or low-income families. This raises a caution flag for those who claim that living wage ordinances are likely to help reduce urban poverty. However, as pointed out repeatedly, these results for minimum wages do not necessarily generalize to living wage ordinances, which differ from standard minimum wage increases in potentially important ways. Aside from possible differences in their effects on employment and wages, their effects on the distribution of family incomes can also differ, depending on who gains and who loses from living wages and the family's overall income. The effects of living wages could be quite different from those of minimum wages, in particular if relatively more of the winners from living wages are workers in low-income families.

---

[3]In addition, O'Brien-Strain and MaCurdy (2000), using data from California, suggest that higher prices stemming from minimum wage increases fall more heavily on low-income families.

4. Existing Research on Living Wages

Living wages are a recent phenomenon. As a consequence, little empirical research has been conducted on their effects.[1] Most important, no one has attempted a systematic empirical evaluation of the actual effects of living wage laws on low-wage workers and their families.

Labor Market Effects

The best-known work on living wages is Pollin and Luce (1998, hereafter PL), which is based on their evaluation of the Los Angeles living wage proposal. Their primary purpose was to advocate living wages as a viable poverty-fighting tool. This work is a useful starting point for research on the subject, because it is cited often and because calculations similar to those they used have been employed by others evaluating living wage proposals in other cities.

Two central arguments of PL's work are (1) that living wage ordinances will deliver a higher standard of living for low-income families, and (2) that such legislation will reduce government subsidy payments to working families. To support these two claims, they present a calculation for a typical Los Angeles family of four with a single wage earner who experiences a wage gain equal to the change from the California minimum wage to the Los Angeles living wage. In their calculation, the family's disposable income increases by $2,500 per year, and as a result of their higher income, the value of the food stamps and Medicaid that they receive declines and their EITC becomes smaller.

---

[1]In addition, most of the existing research–rather than being entirely objective and disinterested–has been by conducted by researchers or organizations that advocate a particular position with regard to living wages and has not been published in peer-reviewed academic publications.

Additionally, they argue that these benefits will occur with relatively small added labor costs to firms.[2]

There are several problems with this work from the perspective of analyzing the effectiveness of living wage policies. First, the authors' calculations are based on a typical Los Angeles family, but they admit that only 42 percent of those earning a wage at or below the Los Angeles living wage are the single wage earners in a family. Moreover, the average family size for these workers is 2.1, indicating that on average workers are not supporting a family of four on living wages. Thus, PL's estimates of disposable income gains cannot be read as expected effects of living wages on families of four with a single worker earning a low wage. These same facts imply that their estimates of reductions in government benefits to workers affected by the living wage are not representative, as these benefits are conditional on the number of dependents and on the incomes of other workers in the family.

Second, the calculations are hypothetical, based on ex ante calculations rather than on data from before and after the passage of living wage ordinances. Since the work grew out of an evaluation of a living wage proposal for Los Angeles, there was, of course, no way to measure the observed effects, so this is not a criticism of their approach per se. However, policy recommendations in the absence of such before

---

[2]To measure the added labor costs per firm, PL begin with a list of contractor firms classified by industry. They then use Current Population Survey (CPS) Outgoing Rotation Group (ORG) files to determine the percentage of workers in an industry that would be affected by a living wage (i.e., those earning below the Los Angeles living wage) and employer data to estimate the average number of employees per firm in the same industries. Merging this information allows them to calculate a per-firm average number of workers who would be affected by a living wage increase, and, thus, the increase in labor costs per covered firm. Of course, the distribution of costs across firms may be quite uneven, so that some firms (e.g., contractors with a low-wage workforce) would likely experience large cost increases.

In addition, PL use interviews with three Los Angeles employers that paid employees relatively high wages before the living wage ordinance was passed to show that paying a high wage to workers may be beneficial to firms. Specifically, the interviews suggest that worker turnover and absenteeism is lower because the firms' workers are happier receiving higher wages than their counterparts at other firms. This evidence is purely anecdotal, however. These firms are likely already paying their workers higher wages because such a strategy earns them higher profits, and thus their experience does not necessarily predict what would happen to other firms if external legislation mandated raising wages.

and after evidence are unwarranted or at least very risky. Furthermore, given the accumulating experience of cities with living wage laws, there is no longer any reason to rely on such ex ante evaluations for assessing their effects.

Most important, PL do not attempt to estimate whether living wages lead to employment or hours reductions, nor do they assume any such effects. It is no surprise that a calculation based on raising the wages of low-wage workers while assuming no reduction in employment or hours worked will look beneficial to low-wage workers. But if either decline as a result of a living wage increase, some families could suffer income declines. PL cite only Card and Krueger's (1994) work specifically in concluding that living wages have no employment effects. They also state that "Numerous other studies, examining the detailed changes in specific labor markets throughout the country due to an increase in the minimum wage, have produced results similar to those in Card and Krueger's analysis of New Jersey and Pennsylvania" (p. 41). However, given that much recent evidence contradicts Card and Krueger's findings (most directly Neumark and Wascher, 2000), the possibility cannot be dismissed that workers will face reduced employment or work hours as a result of living wage ordinances. For all of these reasons, PL's work cannot be viewed as reliable empirical evidence on the effects of living wages on low-income families.

Despite the fact that PL's approach and calculations cannot serve as a basis for reliably evaluating the effects of living wages, their calculations have been used to evaluate ordinances in New Orleans, Miami-Dade County, and Detroit, among other cities. Not surprisingly, since these evaluations are based on the same assumptions used by PL, they reach similar conclusions. For example, Reynolds (1999) argues that the costs to employers operating under a city contract in Detroit would increase by 5 percent to 9 percent of the cost of the contract. For those receiving financial assistance as part of the Empowerment Zones program or the Industrial Facilities Tax Exemption, the added costs would be under 1 percent of the firm's annual budget. Reynolds asserts that, although the costs are small, a financial benefit would accrue to about 2,300 Detroit workers who would each see annual income gains for their families of between $1,300 and $4,400. Reynolds claims that the benefits outweigh the costs, although the basis for this claim is unclear.

There have been attempts to predict the loss of jobs that will result from living wages. For instance, two studies use existing estimates from the minimum wage literature and apply them to living wages. Tolley et al. (1999) report that over 1,300 jobs will be lost in Chicago from the city's living wage ordinance.[3] Recall the point made above, though, that empirical estimates from minimum wage studies may not carry over to living wages. The Employment Policies Institute (1999) estimates that if all of California adopted a statewide living wage, more than 600,000 jobs and $8.3 billion in income would be lost. These calculations assume that every firm in California would be subject to a living wage law despite the fact that no such laws exist (or are even in the planning stages), nor do any current city and county ordinances cover all workers.

In addition to the specific shortcomings of each study mentioned thus far, the unifying problem (already discussed with reference to PL's work) is that they fail to study what has actually happened in localities where living wages have been adopted and are based in large part on conjectures. Two exceptions are a study of the Los Angeles living wage by Sander and Lokey (1998) and a study of the effects of the Detroit living wage law on nonprofits (Reynolds, 2000). Although both provide valuable information, they are essentially case studies, precluding generalizations and missing a control group with which to compare experiences to try to gauge the independent effects of living wage laws.

Contracting

Two studies look at living wage effects after adoption of legislation, focusing on the contracting side. They consider the experiences of Baltimore, the first city to adopt a living wage. Weisbrot and Sforza-Roderick (1996), who review the costs of and bidding for city contracts through an analysis of 23 matched pairs of pre-living wage and post-

---

[3]They also estimate that the cost to the city will be near $20 million per year, including enforcement costs of $4.2 million. The latter figure comes from the Office of Management and Budget. Some figures reported by Los Angeles and Baltimore suggest enforcement costs well under $1 million (Reynolds, 1999), whereas Sander and Lokey (1998) estimate enforcement costs in Los Angeles of about $1 million annually.

living wage contracts in Baltimore, conclude that the real cost of city contracts actually declined as a result of living wage ordinances, thus apparently debunking a central argument of living wage opponents.[4] There was also a small decline in the number of bids per contract, but this was not statistically significant. The estimated costs of monitoring and enforcement were small as well. Niedt et al. (1999) conducted a second study of the effects of the Baltimore living wage ordinance and arrived at similar conclusions to those of Weisbrot and Sforza-Roderick (1996) in regard to cost increases for cities and the number of bids per contract.[5] A critique of this study by the Employment Policies Institute (1998) questions these results. Among the many problems cited, it is claimed that one of the 23 contracts matched by Weisbrot and Sforza-Roderick was just an extension of a pre-existing contract and not subject to the living wage law. Additionally, many contracts considered as post-living wage contracts actually started before the law went into effect. Finally, bid information was overstated. The institute's study claims that correcting all of these errors reverses the findings of the study.

Although the effect of living wages on contracting costs is important, these studies are quite limited. In particular, because they focus on one city, there is no "control sample" of cities in which living wages did not increase with which to compare the changes in contracting costs for Baltimore. Coupled with the ambiguities regarding the results of Baltimore's living wage, the effect of living wage laws on contracting costs remains an open question.

Living Wage Reports for California

A number of reports have been written for California cities when these cities were contemplating raising their living wages. These studies

---

[4]Although the authors provide no evidence regarding the effects on the wages of workers or the incomes of families, they do state that employment levels did not change as a result of the living wage ordinance. They base the claim solely on interviews with 31 firms conducted shortly after the passage of the legislation.

[5]They also suggest that there has been a financial gain for a few workers, but they do not quantify this gain or apply any estimation technique to arrive at this conclusion. They argue that, according to interviews with workers, there has been no reduction in employment. Once again, however, no attempt is made to estimate a direct effect of the living wage on low-wage workers or low-income families.

include Alunan et al. (1999) and Reich et al. (1999) for San Francisco; Reich and Hall (1999) for the Airport and Port of San Francisco; Williams and Sander (1997) for Los Angeles; Williams (1998) for San Jose; and Zabin et al. (1999) for the Port of Oakland. Finally, Sander et al. (2000) and Pollin and Brenner (2000) have written reports regarding the living wage in Santa Monica, which is due to be implemented in 2002. The Santa Monica proposal, however, is part minimum wage and part living wage, applying to private sector employers (of a certain size in prime business zones) irrespective of whether they have contracts with or business assistance from the city.

These studies all suffer from the limitations of most of the other studies described above in that they attempt to estimate how cities might be affected but look only at data before the implementation of living wages, rather than looking at data before and after to assess the actual effects. Of course, as noted above, in the case of a city contemplating implementing a living wage, this is all that can be done. Thus, this is not intended as a criticism of these studies on methodological grounds. Rather, it is meant simply to point out the main contribution of the research in this monograph, which is to assess evidence on the actual effects of living wages.

Despite their limitations, the existing reports for California cities are of some interest. Their most interesting feature is their attempts to determine who might be affected by living wage laws covering city contractors, using a variety of approaches including independent surveys. Some of the resulting estimates were reported in Table 1.1. In contrast, the information in the data analyzed in this monograph does not permit the identification of covered workers. On the other hand, living wage effects may well spill over to uncovered workers, and—as indicated below—sometimes more workers are covered by business assistance provisions of living wage laws. Thus, in a policy analysis asking how low-wage workers or low-income families are affected, it is inappropriate—even in the case of contractor-only laws—to focus only on those who are covered by dint of employment with city contractors. Nonetheless, insofar as cities contemplating living wage increases are interested in trying to assess the likely immediate cost effects on contractors (assuming no other cost-reducing responses), these reports may prove to be helpful. A thorough evaluation of their methods for estimating covered contractor employment and their resulting findings is beyond the scope of this monograph.

Summary

This review suggests a need for considerably more analysis of the effects of living wage ordinances on workers and families, focusing on the actual experiences of cities where living wages have been enacted. Proponents of the living wage make strong claims that poverty will be reduced, and opponents make strong claims that some low-wage workers will lose their jobs, possibly increasing poverty. Empirical evidence is required to resolve these questions. This monograph is intended to make a substantive contribution in this direction, and the next four chapters present the main empirical evidence.

5. Do Living Wage Laws Raise the Wages of Low-Wage Workers?

This chapter takes a first step in research assessing the effects of living wages. In particular, it attempts to establish whether the first-order effect of living wages is increased wages of low-wage workers. Although this is the anticipated effect, these effects may not be observed. First, there is no existing research documenting the extent of compliance with living wage laws (in contrast to minimum wage laws; see Ashenfelter and Smith, 1979), and it is conceivable that they are largely ignored or not enforced. Viewed from this perspective, a failure to find wage effects should push researchers and policymakers to study the implementation and enforcement of living wage laws.

Second, because living wage laws appear to be targeted toward a very narrow group of workers, it may be impossible to detect living wage effects using standard datasets—in particular, the CPS—that labor economists and other researchers use to study policies with geographic variation (for example, the minimum wage, but also welfare or other income-support programs, anti-discrimination legislation, and unemployment insurance). This would suggest that such datasets may not be useful in evaluating the effects of living wage laws. Instead, researchers may have to rely on ex ante calculations, such as the city-specific reports and other studies have done, or perhaps on surveys or case studies designed explicitly to study workers and firms affected by living wage laws. This would be unfortunate, as the CPS provides data covering essentially all metropolitan areas in the United States, permitting generalizations to be drawn, providing control group cities where living wages were not implemented, and readily allowing comparisons with other policies in effect at the same or different times.

On the other hand, if living wage laws are seen to have a positive effect on the wages of low-wage workers, we would conclude that such laws are effective. Furthermore, given the low estimates of coverage by the most common type of living wage law–namely, the coverage of city contractors–we would be led to ask why living wage laws may have broader effects than suggested by the narrow coverage estimates.

Data

Information on living wages was presented in Chapter 1. Although a few such laws were passed in 1996 or earlier, most came into effect after 1996. For this reason, and because cities cannot be identified in the dataset for a period in 1995, much of the analysis is restricted to 1996 and after.[1] Not all of the living wage laws listed in Tables 1.1 to 1.3 are used in this empirical analysis because some of the smaller municipalities (and therefore residents of them) cannot be identified,[2] whereas others can be identified but do not provide enough observations to permit reliable statistical analyses.[3] The latter case is not problematic; because the analysis focuses only on individuals and families in larger municipalities, the inability to identify the small municipalities with living wage laws does not result in misclassifying workers as residing in cities without living wage laws when in fact they do.

Data on wages, additional labor market outcomes considered in subsequent chapters, and other worker-related characteristics are drawn from the CPS ORG files extending from January 1996 through December 2000. These files identify residents of metropolitan statistical areas encompassing all large- and medium-sized cities in the United States. However, to draw reliable inferences, this analysis is restricted to larger cities for which a sufficient number of observations is available (as detailed below). Since January 1996, the design of the CPS has resulted

---

[1]Specifically, city codes are unavailable for the ORGs of the CPS for part of 1995 because of the phasing in of a new sample based on the 1990 Census.

[2]These include Berkeley, Cambridge, Corvallis, Duluth, Hayward, Pasadena, San Fernando, Santa Cruz, Somerville, Warren, West Hollywood, and Ypsilanti.

[3]The set of cities included based on this criterion varies, depending on which analysis is being conducted.

in the large- and medium-sized metropolitan areas in the sample being self-representing (Bureau of the Census, 1997).[4] This is yet another reason for using information only from January 1996 and after.

Data on residents of these metropolitan areas are extracted for the empirical analysis, and living wages are assigned to these residents according to the major city in the metropolitan area (e.g., Los Angeles in the Los Angeles-Long Beach metropolitan area). This assignment of living wages poses a couple of limitations. First, assignment of people to a metropolitan area according to where they live, rather than where they work, is appropriate if we are interested—as a policy matter—in how a living wage law affects residents of a city. However, classifying people by where they work might better reveal the direct effects of living wage laws, especially insofar as employees of firms covered by living wage laws work in the city. Second, the correspondence between cities and metropolitan areas is imperfect. In many cases, the metropolitan area will include some suburban areas, but because suburban residents may work in the city, and because employers covered by living wage laws do not necessarily hire only city residents, this is not necessarily inappropriate.[5] However, it seems likely that some fraction of residents of metropolitan areas are not affected by living wage laws, which implies that the coverage estimates reported in Chapter 1 overstate somewhat the fraction of covered workers in the metropolitan area. An additional complication is posed by small municipalities within a metropolitan area that have their own living wage (such as West Hollywood or Berkeley). Because residents of (and workers in) these smaller municipalities cannot be identified, this potentially introduces some measurement error into the prevailing living wage, although it is likely to be relatively minor because of the small share of the workforce covered, relative to the laws of the larger municipalities, and because these living wage laws at least sometimes echo those of the larger city in the metropolitan area (e.g.,

---

[4]In a few cases, outlying counties are excluded from the CPS sampling frame for a metropolitan area, in which case the data are representative of the remainder of the metropolitan area.

[5]For expositional ease, the text often refers to cities rather than metropolitan areas.

West Hollywood and Los Angeles implemented the same living wage in 1997, although in different months).

An alternative is to use the CPS Annual Demographic Files (ADFs), which have data on family earnings and income. The ORGs are preferable for looking at effects on wages, employment, and hours. First, as Tables 1.1 through 1.3 show, there is variation in the months in which living wage ordinances pass. Reliance on the ADFs would restrict the data to a single "reading" per year and would thereby sacrifice some of the variation in living wages across observations. Second, the ADFs would give us fewer observations overall. Although the ORGs provide information on wages for only one-fourth of the sample, the data are available in each month, and thus the ORGs provide a sample three times as large. Third, the ADFs are released slowly, whereas the monthly ORG files are released quickly. For example, the March 2000 ADF was not released until the fall of 2000. In addition, the March files cover the previous year, so it is not possible to study the consequences of living wage ordinances put into place in 2000 until the data for March 2001 are released.

On the other hand, the ADFs are preferable for looking at the effects of living wages on family income or on poverty. First, the ADFs allow more accurate measurement of family income (because unearned family income information is included) and better classification of families as poor (because the income data are annual). Second, with the ADFs, it is possible to match families and their income information to city living wage information dating from 1995. This is because family income information in 1995 is reported in the 1996 ADF, for which metropolitan area codes are available. Finally, there is no monthly poverty threshold, so one can either choose some arbitrary method of interpolating annual thresholds by month or face differences in poverty rates driven by the month of the year from which monthly data are drawn. For these reasons, the ADFs serve as the primary data source for the estimates of the effects of living wages on poverty (see Chapter 7).

Table 5.1 lists the key variables used in the various empirical analyses. Those constructed from the CPS ORG files are listed first, followed by those constructed from the ADFs. These are followed by policy variables and other variables necessary for the statistical analysis. The manner in which these variables are used is described below.

Table 5.1

Variables Used in the Analysis of the Effects of Living Wages

Variable	Definition/Construction
CPS ORG Variables	
Hourly wage	Earnings per hour for hourly workers; usual weekly earnings/usual hours at main job per week for everyone else
Hours worked	Usual hours worked per week at main job
Employment	Dummy variable set = 1 if individual currently has a job; = 0 otherwise
Individual earnings	Estimated annual earnings for an individual assuming a full year of work
CPS ADF Variables	
Total family earnings	Sum of annual earnings of each family member
Total family income	Combined earned and unearned income of each family member
Policy Variables	
Minimum wage	The minimum wage effective on the first of the month in the state in which the metropolitan area is located (weighted average of minimums if metropolitan area straddles states)
Living wage	The living wage effective in a metropolitan area
Poverty threshold	The yearly income determined by the U.S. Census Bureau below which a family with a given number of adults and children are in poverty
Other Variables	
Year dummy variables	Separate dummy variables for each year from 1996 to 1999
Month dummy variables	Separate dummy variables for each calendar month (11)
Metropolitan area dummy variables	Separate dummy variables for each metropolitan area

Overall Research Design

This chapter looks at wage effects. However, the research design for examining the wage, hours worked, employment, earnings, and income effects of living wage ordinances is often similar, so some general discussion that applies to the following chapters as well is presented in this and the next four subsections.

In all cases, outcomes for workers and families in cities passing living wage laws are compared with earlier outcomes in the same cities in the period before the living wage was passed (or increased). The earlier period controls for "city effects." That is, this comparison with the earlier period avoids attributing to living wages what may simply be a fixed characteristic—e.g., a lower poverty rate—of a city. In addition, it is critical to avoid attributing to living wage laws the effects of other changes (such as aggregate economic activity) occurring over time. Thus, changes in cities passing living wage laws are compared with changes over the same time span in a control group of cities that did not pass such laws, so that only the relative changes in the same period that are associated with living wage laws are causally attributed to such laws. In other words, because living wage ordinances are not randomly assigned either across geographic locations or the sample period, the research design accounts for the possible correlation of living wage laws with unmeasured influences on labor market outcomes that vary across the cities or years in the sample. This is called a "difference-in-differences" research design, because it infers the effects of living wages from the difference between outcomes in cities passing (or increasing) living wages before and after their implementation, relative to the difference in outcomes over the same period for cities not passing (or not increasing) living wages.[6]

---

[6]The analysis ignores living wages in counties that are distinct from cities (currently on the books in 14 counties in California, Florida, Illinois, New Jersey, Oregon, Pennsylvania, Texas, and Wisconsin). In many cases, the counties covered are small and, in general, county living wage laws have not attracted a great deal of attention, perhaps because the number of workers covered may be quite low. In the analysis in this monograph, county living wage laws are relevant only if they cover workers in cities included in the dataset but classified as not having living wage laws. The only county living wage law that clearly covers a city included in those we study is in Miami-Dade County. In general, this problem should bias any estimated effects of city living wage

Analyzing Wage Effects

We begin the analysis by asking whether there is evidence that living wage laws succeed in boosting the wages of low-wage workers. If they do not, of course, then it is unlikely that any positive (or negative) effects will flow from them. This may seem like a trivial question, with the answer certain to be in the affirmative, but indeed there is virtually no research documenting the extent of compliance with these laws.[7] In contrast, compliance with standard minimum wage laws has been studied and documented (Ashenfelter and Smith, 1979), as have the effects of minimum wages on the wage distribution (e.g., Neumark et al., 1999). Furthermore, as noted above, there is the question of whether these wage effects can be detected in representative samples. The following discussion presents a detailed analysis of wage effects but also discusses general issues that arise in drawing causal inferences from the empirical estimates, thereby providing a more in-depth discussion of the research design that applies to the other outcomes examined in this monograph.

To begin the study of living wage effects, a wage equation is estimated for various ranges of the wage distribution in cities. Specifically, the estimation is done for workers falling at or below the 10th centile (i.e., those in the bottom tenth of the wage distribution), between the 10th and 25th centiles, between the 25th and 50th centiles, and between the 50th and 75th centiles of their city's wage distribution in a particular month. This wage equation asks, quite simply, whether the average wages of workers in a particular part of the wage distribution in a metropolitan area increase as a result of living wage laws. Of course, much of the emphasis is on answering this question for workers in the lowest part of the distribution.

---

laws toward zero, as the control group may actually include some individuals subject to living wages. Thus, the effects of living wage laws that are reported in this and subsequent chapters may be understated. But given the large number of cities in the control group, this problem should be negligible, which was verified in estimates not reported in the tables in which Miami was excluded.

[7]Compliance may be an issue because of a lag between initial passage of an ordinance and the adoption and dissemination of guidelines to contractors and others and the establishment of an apparatus to verify and enforce compliance. Sander and Lokey (1998) provide case study evidence from Los Angeles indicating slow but increasing progress toward compliance.

The sample is restricted to workers with an hourly wage greater than $1.00 but less than or equal to $100 and to those between the ages of 16 and 70, inclusive. To improve accuracy, the analysis is also restricted to city-month cells with 25 or more observations.[8] Pooling data across months, the following regression is estimated for each centile range:

$$\ln(w_{icmy}) = \alpha + X_{icmy}\omega + \beta \ln(w_{cmy}^{min})$$
$$+ \gamma \max[\ln(w_{cmy}^{liv}), \ln(w_{cmy}^{min})] + Y_y \delta_Y \qquad (5.1)$$
$$+ M_m \delta_M + C_c \delta_C + \varepsilon_{icmy},$$

where w is the hourly wage, X is a set of demographic control variables,[9] w^{min} is the higher of the federal or state minimum wage,[10] w^{liv} is the living wage, and the equation is estimated separately for each specified centile range. The subscripts i, c, m, and y denote individual, city, month, and year. Y, M, and C are vectors of year, month, and city dummy variables (with regression coefficients δ_Y, δ_M, and δ_C), and ε is a random error term.[11]

Note that explicit controls for local labor market conditions, such as the unemployment rate or employment rate, are not included. Although local labor market conditions can surely matter, they are also potentially endogenous if, for example, living wages cause some job loss. The year and month dummy variables capture changes in economic conditions at the aggregate level, and the city dummy variables control for city-specific differences. However, a potential problem arises if economic conditions are changing differentially by location. As an alternative (discussed

---

[8]The cities included in the wage analysis are below listed in Table 5.4.

[9]These include controls for age, gender, race, educational attainment, and marital status.

[10]In the few cases of metropolitan areas that straddle states with different minimum wages (Davenport-Quad Cities, Philadelphia, Portland, and Providence), a weighted average of the minimum wages in the two states is used, weighted by the shares of the metropolitan area population in each state (averaged over the months of 1996).

[11]For all the specifications reported in this monograph, less restrictive models were also estimated using unique dummy variables for each month in the sample (so, for example, for two years of data, the model would include 23 unique monthly dummy variables instead of one year dummy variable and 11 calendar month dummy variables). The estimates were virtually unchanged and the substantive conclusions unaffected.

below), the cities passing living wage laws in the sample period are allowed in some specifications to have different (linear) trends. This will not capture every possible variation in local economic conditions, but it will capture systematic differences between the two types of cities in the rates of change of wages and the other dependent variables that are studied. Finally, despite reservations regarding potential endogeneity, we estimated the specifications reported below including the overall employment rate for the city-month cell. The conclusions were unaffected.

The living wage variable that multiplies γ is specified as the maximum of the (log of the) living wage and the minimum wage. In the sample period, living wages—when they exist—always exceed minimum wages, so this variable imposes the minimum as the wage floor in the absence of a living wage.[12] It is essential to control for minimum wages because some cities with living wages are in states with high minimum wages, and it is the independent effects of living wages that are of interest. If living wages boost the wages of low-wage workers, positive estimates of γ would be expected when looking at workers in relatively low ranges of the wage distribution. Finally, specifications are also estimated with w^{min} and w^{liv} lagged by six or 12 months to allow for a slower, adaptive response to changes in minimum wages and living wages. In the minimum wage literature, attempts are often made to adjust the minimum wage variable by an estimated coverage rate. That would be appropriate for both the living wage variable and the minimum wage variable (with the latter picking up the fraction of workers covered by the minimum wage but not the living wage). However, as already noted, reliable information on coverage by living wage laws is not available.

Wage effects are estimated for particular ranges of the wage distribution. To better understand the interpretation of the resulting estimates, as well as some potential problems posed by restricting the analysis to a particular range, consider the analysis on which the most

---

[12]We could also specify the living wage variable as the gap between the living wage and the minimum wage. The coefficient on the living wage variable is insensitive to this transformation.

attention is focused—specifically, that of individuals with wages falling below the 10th centile of the wage distribution.[13] The simplest case is one in which some workers below the 10th centile have their wages raised as the result of a living wage law but remain below the 10th centile, and there are no disemployment effects. In such a case, estimation of Eq. (5.1) will show higher average wages of those below the 10th centile for city-month cells following living wage increases. In particular, the estimated effect will equal approximately the average wage gain experienced by those workers whose wages rose because of the living wage, multiplied by the share of workers below the 10th centile whose wages were increased. If we add the possibility of disemployment effects, so that some workers experience wage gains and others become nonemployed, then the estimates will still reveal wage gains. As workers initially below the 10th centile "drop out," the 10th centile rises as the bottom tenth of the workforce now reaches higher into the wage distribution, which itself increases the average wage of those below the 10th centile.[14] Finally, if some workers who are affected by a living wage have their wage increased to a point above the 10th centile, the estimated effect will still be positive, as—paralleling the previous argument—the 10th centile is increased. Indeed, even if all affected workers have their wage increased to a point above the 10th centile, the average wage of those at or below the 10th centile increases; as low-wage workers are "cleared out" from below the 10th centile, the 10th centile increases, and the bottom tenth of the wage distribution is therefore made up of higher-wage workers on average.[15]

---

[13]In all cases, this refers to wages equal to or less than the 10th centile.

[14]Indeed, it is possible in principle, although unlikely, for a disemployment effect to account for the entire estimated wage effect, in which case any wage gains identified by this empirical strategy would not be viewed as salutary. The analysis of poverty effects in Chapter 7, however, speaks directly to the question of income gains taking account of both wage increases and employment losses, as well as other changes.

[15]To see this in a simple example, suppose there are initially 50 workers, with five earning a wage of $5, 20 earning $6, and 25 earning $7. The 10th centile (the wage of the fifth worker from the bottom when workers are ranked by wages) is $5. Now let one worker's wage go from $5 to $7. In this case, the 10th centile rises to $6, as the bottom tenth of the wage distribution now includes four workers earning $5 and one worker earning $6, and the average wage of workers at or below the 10th centile rises from $5 to $5.20. (Furthermore, the average wage increase in the bottom tenth of the wage

However, this discussion emphasizes that the empirical strategy used does not look at changes over time in wages paid to the same individuals, distinguished by their initial wage and whether they were affected by a living wage law. Rather, the strategy asks whether the average wages of workers in a particular part of the wage distribution in a metropolitan area (in the example discussed in this paragraph, the lowest tenth of the distribution) are increased as a result of living wage laws. An alternative is to use the predicted wage distribution, although this would be expected to identify less accurately workers likely to be affected by a living wage law, because, for example, some workers with low observable skills earn high wages. It was verified, nonetheless, that the basic wage results reported in this chapter were qualitatively unchanged using the predicted wage distribution to identify low-wage/low-skilled workers.

It is important to remember that Eq. (5.1) estimates an average effect of living wages for all workers in the specified range of the wage distribution. Even in the lower ranges, though, only a fraction of the workforce is covered. Since effects tend to work in the opposite directions for covered and uncovered workers, as explained in Chapter 2, the estimates from Eq. (5.1), and similar employment estimates described in the next chapter, most likely understate the effects on covered workers in isolation. Of course, from a policy perspective, unless there is some reason to be concerned with covered workers per se, the average effects are probably of most interest.

Finally, it is of some interest to know which types of workers are the focus of attention when looking at particular ranges of the skill distribution, in particular the lowest decile. To this end, Table 5.2 reports the average characteristics of those in this decile compared with those in the rest of the sample. The first column shows these averages for all workers. Those in the lowest decile are considerably younger on average, more likely to be non-white and female, much more likely to be high school dropouts and much less likely to be college graduates, and much more likely to be never married but to come from larger households (presumably because many still live with their parents). The

---

distribution can exceed the average increase in the 10th–25th centile range, as it does in this example.)

Table 5.2

Selected Characteristics of Those Below the 10th Centile of the Imputed Wage Distribution and Those in the Rest of the Sample

	Below the 10th Centile/Rest of Sample						
	All	East	Midwest	South	West	1996	2000
Age	24.05/	25.02/	22.76/	24.40/	23.85/	24.38/	23.70/
	41.35	42.04	41.44	41.28	40.75	41.14	41.55
Race							
White	72.08/	72.42/	74.83/	66.42/	76.77/	71.69/	72.45/
	81.39	82.20	84.69	78.09	82.02	81.80	80.86
Black	20.23/	21.47/	21.05/	29.39/	6.54/	20.74/	19.71/
	12.99	13.17	12.61	18.78	5.85	12.91	13.25
Other	7.69/	6.12/	4.12/	4.19/	16.69/	7.57/	7.83/
	5.62	4.63	2.70	3.13	12.13	5.28	5.89
Gender							
Male	32.55/	31.17/	32.94/	33.66/	32.01/	32.08/	33.10/
	50.93	50.35	51.05	50.63	51.71	50.85	50.91
Female	67.45/	68.83/	67.06/	66.34/	67.99/	67.92/	66.90/
	49.07	49.65	48.95	49.73	48.29	49.15	49.09
Education							
Dropout	71.96/	69.47/	69.60/	72.65/	75.31/	72.58/	71.79/
	11.12	10.41	8.75	11.73	13.00	11.73	10.56
High school	28.04/	30.52/	30.40/	27.35/	24.67/	27.41/	28.19/
	60.10	58.67	63.05	60.38	58.52	60.60	59.70
College	0.01/	0.01/	0/	0/	0.01/	0.003/	0.02/
	28.78	30.93	28.20	27.88	28.48	27.67	29.73
Marital status							
Married	10.02/	8.15/	7.32/	10.46/	13.44/	10.80/	9.67/
	60.66	59.11	61.63	61.61	60.03	61.29	60.11
Separated/	3.88/	3.54/	3.10/	4.50/	4.03/	4.11/	3.51/
divorced	13.03	11.45	12.69	14.19	13.25	12.88	13.03
Widowed	3.72/	4.30/	3.13/	4.11/	3.18/	3.95/	3.45/
	2.52	2.89	2.52	2.54	2.15	2.66	2.48
Never married	82.39/	84.01/	86.45/	80.92/	79.35/	81.14/	83.36/
	23.79	26.55	23.16	21.66	24.57	23.18	24.38
Household size	4.18/	4.11/	4.12/	3.96/	4.58/	4.15/	4.26/
	3.09	3.10	3.04	2.99	3.24	3.09	3.10

NOTE: Means are reported for continuous variables and percentages for all other variables. The regression used to impute wages included controls for education, age (up to a cubic), race, gender, marital status, number of family members, number of children under age 18, year, and interview month.

next four columns break these out by Census region; the patterns are generally quite similar. Finally, the last two columns report these averages for the first and last year of the sample period; there is relatively little change over what is admittedly a quite short interval.

Graphical Analysis

Before presenting the regression results, it is informative to examine some graphical displays of the data. Two such displays are presented in Figures 5.1 and 5.2. These figures are helpful in understanding how the data are used in the empirical analysis and in providing a "broad-brush" view of the evidence.

Figure 5.1 plots information on average log wages in the lower decile of the wage distribution, and the living wage variable (the maximum of the minimum and living wage), for cities that are represented in every month of the sample.[16] The first eight graphs are for the living wage cities, and the ninth graph is for the control group cities. The vertical lines in the first eight graphs are for the month in which the living wage was initially implemented. The solid lines in the graphs are simply the values of the living wage variable. Before implementation of the living wage, these move up slightly, reflecting minimum wage increases. Then, at the date of implementation, the graphs display a large vertical jump, followed by smaller increases in cities where living wages subsequently rose. Finally, the dashed lines capture changes in average wages in the lower decile. These wages were first deflated by the average hourly earnings index, with the beginning of 1996 used as a base. Then for each of the living wage cities, the deflated average wage was regressed on a time trend and a dummy variable indicating that a living wage law was in effect. The fitted value from this regression is plotted. Thus, the slope of the line in each graph indicates the trend in real wages in the lower decile, and the discrete shift (if there is one) captures the average difference, net of this trend, in the pre- and post–living wage period. In the last graph–for the control cities–only the overall trend is plotted.

---

[16]That is, these cities have at least 25 observations in every month. Of course, numerous other cities meet this criterion for many but not all months and therefore contribute to the regression analysis.

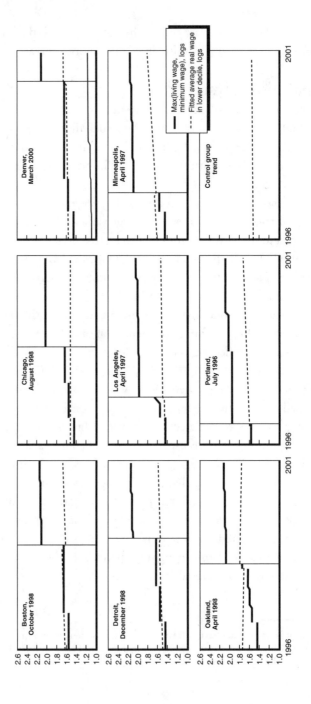

Figure 5.1—Log Wages

48

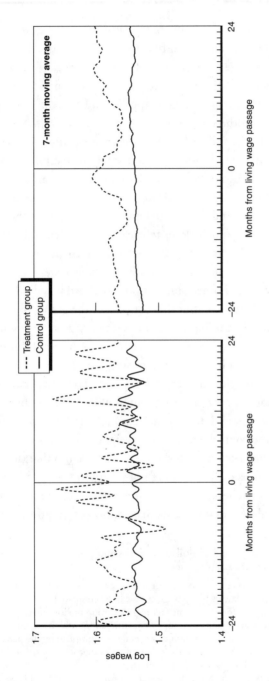

Figure 5.2—Event Analysis, Wages

The dashed lines in the graphs show that in four of the cities (Denver, Los Angeles, Oakland, and Portland), wages shifted up following the living wage increase, whereas in three cities (Boston, Detroit, and Minneapolis) a downward shift (smaller on average) is detected, and in Chicago no change is apparent. Thus, the evidence is not unambiguously in the same direction for every city. Note, though, that in these graphs, the shift is forced to occur at the time the living wage law is implemented. In the regression analysis that follows, wage increases are found to occur with a lag of about one year, and if the graphs reflected this, the evidence of wage increases would be stronger.

Figure 5.2 goes beyond the largest cities and summarizes the data for the full sample, coming much closer to the answers provided by the regression analysis. This graph presents what is called an "event analysis." In particular, for each city passing a living wage, the month of passage is set to zero, and other observations are dated based on the number of months before or after this period. In the graph, observations are displayed up to 24 months before and after passage of the living wage law, when such observations are available.[17] Thus, the graph for living wage cities shows the evolution of average wages in the lower decile of the wage distribution before and after living wage laws are passed. Constructing a graph for the control group is a bit more complex; since no living wage law is passed, there is no natural "zero" date for these cities. Thus, for the control group cities, weighted averages of observations are constructed, with the weights chosen so that the distribution of months included in each observation (from −24 to 24) for the control group matches that for the same month for the treatment group.[18] As a result, for example, the distribution of months used to

---

[17]Fewer observations would be available if, for example, a living wage law was passed toward the end of the sample period.

[18]More specifically, to create a control set of data points to which the effect before and after the passage of the law in living wage cities can be compared, the average log wage variable is constructed for each month among the group of cities that never passed a living wage. Then, to create a data point for a "constructed month" 24 months before the passage of a law, for example, each month's average is multiplied by the percentage of observations that the month takes up in the group of cities that will pass a law 24 months later. This is done for each month, with the sum then taken over all months. Since this is two years before passage of the laws, all observations for 1999–2000 will have zero

construct the observation at –24 for the control group matches that for the treatment group. Two graphs are shown–one for the monthly data, and one for a seven-month moving average, with the reference month as the midpoint to smooth the data.

Looking at the smoothed data in the right-hand panel of Figure 5.2, a few things are observed. First, in the period before implementing the living wage, average wages were higher in the treatment group of cities that later pass a living wage law. This is captured in the city dummy variables included in the regression equation. The question is whether the difference grows or shrinks following the implementation of living wage laws. Looking at the months after implementation, it appears that the difference grows. After about 12 months have passed, the gap between living wage and non-living wage cities begins to grow, ending up larger than it was before the implementation of living wage laws. Of course, the regression analysis pins down these features in more detail and allows for a more refined analysis (such as allowing different trends in living wage and non-living wage cities). However, Figure 5.2 displays the basic features of the data and reveals approximately the same answer as does the regression analysis described below–that with a lag of about one year, living wages increase the wages of the lowest-wage workers.

Basic Wage Results

The results for Eq. (5.1) are reported in Table 5.3; all coefficient estimates and standard errors are multiplied by 100. The table reveals no contemporaneous effects of living wages for any of the centile ranges (specification 1). Six months after a living wage increase, there are still no significant effects detected, although the estimated coefficients are all positive and larger than in the contemporaneous specification. However, at a lag of one year, there are positive and significant effects for the 0th–10th centile range. The coefficient of 6.95 means that the elasticity of average wages in this wage range with respect to changes in the living

---

weight in this calculation and will not be used. The same procedure is used for each "constructed month" up to and after the passage of the law. Later "constructed months," such as 24 months after passage, will be heavily weighted toward the later months.

Table 5.3

Effects of Living Wage Laws on Wages, Basic Results

	Centile Range			
	≤ 10	10–25	25–50	50–75
Specification 1:	−0.53	0.27	0.95	−0.03
Living wage	(2.23)	(1.62)	(1.65)	(1.63)
Specification 2:	1.91	0.84	2.22	0.34
Living wage, 6-month lag	(2.25)	(1.70)	(1.76)	(1.79)
Specification 3:	6.95**	0.93	−0.01	−1.08
Living wage, 12-month lag	(2.40)	(1.78)	(1.85)	(1.92)
Sample size	34,435	42,912	71,135	72,737

NOTES: The control group is other urban workers. Each entry is an estimate from a separate specification for log wages. Standard errors are reported in parentheses. All estimates are multiplied by 100 and therefore measure the percentage increase in wages in the specified range that occurs in response to a 100 percent increase in the living wage. For a metropolitan area's data to be included in the sample for a particular month, there must be at least 25 observations in that city-month cell. Observations for which allocated information is required to construct the wage variable in the CPS are dropped. The log wage equation controls for year, month, metropolitan area, education, age, marital status, race, gender, and the minimum wage at the same lag as the living wage variable. The estimates with an 18-month lag are similar to those with a 12-month lag. Reported standard errors are robust to nonindependence (and heteroscedasticity) within city-month cells. A total of 130 cities are used in the analyses.

**Significantly different from zero at the 5 percent level.

wage is approximately 0.07. For example, a 50 percent increase in the living wage (over the minimum wage) would raise average wages for this group by 3.5 percent (6.95 × 0.5). The lagged effect is not unreasonable, because implementation of living wage laws may be a rather drawn-out process and cities often apply the wage floor only when contracts are renewed (as happened, for example, in Baltimore and San Jose). As might be expected, there is no strong evidence of wage effects in the higher centile ranges. In general, then, these data appear to detect wage-increasing effects of living wage ordinances for the lowest-wage workers.[19]

Although the effect of living wages appears in the 12-month lag specification, the (positive) effect of the minimum wage appears in the contemporaneous specification. This raises the possibility that in the 12-month lag specification the omission of the contemporaneous minimum wage biases the estimated living wage effect. However, the results are very similar if the contemporaneous, six-month, and 12-month lags of the living wage and minimum wage variables are included simultaneously, or if the contemporaneous minimum wage variable is added to the specification with the 12-month lags. One might expect the different lags of the same policy variable to be highly collinear but, conditional on city, year, and month fixed effects, they are not.

The sample sizes indicated in Table 5.3 are very large, reflecting the large number of individuals covered in the CPS. However, because living wages vary across city-month cells, each individual-level observation does not really provide "independent" information on the effects of living wages. This problem can be addressed in one of two ways. One approach comes at the problem from a statistical angle, emphasizing that when there are many observations associated with each policy change (i.e., data on many individuals in the same city and month in which a living wage changes), these observations are not independent. If, instead, this were ignored, the standard errors would be artificially

---

[19]The estimates of the minimum wage effects (not reported) indicate stronger effects initially, although they dissipate and become smaller and statistically insignificant in the 12-month lag specification. A natural question is why the minimum wage effects dissipate over time but the living wage effects do not. Given the lags with which living wages increase wages (which, as argued above, is a reasonable expectation), this apparent difference could be solely the result of failure to include longer lags of living wage effects. To check this, although a long panel is not available, lags of 18 and 24 months were added. This resulted in, if anything, slightly stronger positive effects of living wages, so the difference seems real. The simplest explanation is that the slow process of implementing and enforcing compliance with living wage laws means that the growing effects of these influences may offset any diminution of effects paralleling those that arise with minimum wages. This is especially likely to be true in a short panel that to a large extent captures the beginnings of living wage legislation; future data should be able to provide more decisive evidence on this question. It is also possible that because many living wage laws are indexed, employers expect the wage constraint to keep pace with inflation and hence respond differently than to a minimum wage increase.

small, and the results would suggest greater precision of the estimates than is in fact the case. To address this problem, Table 5.3 reports standard errors that relax the assumption of independence within city-month cells.[20]

The second approach is to simply use the data aggregated to the city-month level. To this end, the wage equations were also estimated using the specified wage percentiles for the city (i.e., 10th, 25th, 50th, and 75th) as dependent variables, rather than the individual-level data on individuals in these ranges.[21] The results were very similar to those reported in the tables using individual-level data. The same is true for the analyses reported in subsequent chapters; where individual-level data are used, standard errors accounting for non-independence within city-month cells are reported, and results are very similar using data aggregated to the city-month level.

Additional Research Design Issues

A couple of issues arise in considering the validity of the evidence based on the research design embodied in Eq. (5.1). First, as explained above, the equation uses a difference-in-differences strategy to identify the effects of living wages. In this framework, the effect of living wages—the treatment—is identified from how changes over time in cities implementing (or raising) living wages differ from changes over the same time period in cities without (or not raising) living wages. The difference-in-differences strategy is predicated on the assumption that absent the living wage, and aside from differences captured in the other control variables, the cities that pass living wage laws (the treatment group) are comparable to those that do not pass such laws (the control

---

[20]This procedure also allows for the variance of the error to differ across city-month cells. However, it still assumes that observations are independent across months. These standard errors are calculated using the "cluster" command in Stata. The issue of incorrect standard errors when the data are at a more disaggregated level than is the policy variation is discussed in detail in Moulton (1986).

[21]Because there are different numbers of observations per city-month cell, and estimates should be less precise in cells with fewer observations, the data were weighted by multiplying the observations by $(N_{cmy})^{1/2}$; when the dependent variable is a percentile for a cell rather than a mean, this is the correct weighting scheme as long as the density is the same across cells (Mood et al., 1974).

group). Although fixed differences between cities are handled by the difference-in-differences approach, potentially more troublesome is a difference in the time pattern of changes stemming, for example, from a different prior trend in a dependent variable in the treatment and control groups. Because the specification assumes only fixed city and time effects, with the latter assumed to be the same across all observations, such a difference in the time pattern would tend to be incorrectly attributed to the effects of living wages.

To test whether different time trends in the treatment and control groups may bias the estimates, the sample was restricted to include the control group cities and only the pre-living wage observations on the treatment group cities. Specifications for each dependent variable were then estimated, adding—in addition to the control variable each one includes—a time trend and an interaction between this time trend and a dummy variable for cities later implementing living wages.[22] The estimated coefficient of the time trend interaction provides a test for differential time trends in the treatment and control groups for the dependent variable in question.[23] In all cases—i.e., for wages in this chapter and for the other outcomes studied in subsequent chapters—this estimated coefficient was small and not significantly different from zero, which bolsters the validity of the research design.

This was taken one step further. In particular, for each set of results reported in this monograph, specifications were estimated including the entire sample period, retaining the differential time trends for the treatment and control groups. Even though in these cases it is more difficult to separate the effects of the living wage and the time trend for the treatment group—because living wages invariably grow over the sample period—the estimated effects of living wages on the various outcomes considered were generally similar to those reported in the tables that follow, sometimes a bit stronger and sometimes a bit weaker, but leading to the same qualitative conclusions.

---

[22]The living wage variable was dropped because all observations are taken before the introduction of a living wage.

[23]If dummy variables unique to each sample month were included, only the time trend interaction would be identified and the relevant test would still be whether its coefficient was different from zero.

Second, for the analysis of wages, the choice of a cutoff at the 10th centile is somewhat arbitrary. It was chosen because comparisons of wages of workers at the 50th and 10th centiles are often used in studies of wage inequality assessing relative outcomes for low-wage workers, and also because living wages, although generally above the 10th centile, are often relatively close (see Table 1.4). But if living wage compliance is perfect and there are no effects on the wages of other workers, the fact that many living wages exceed the 10th centile suggests that many workers whose wages are increased as a result of living wage laws will be dropped from the sample using the 10th centile as a cutoff. However, these assumptions are unlikely to hold. Workers may not be paid the living wage for all of their hours of work, compliance (including paying wages below the living wage) may be incomplete,[24] and spillover effects seem likely, so wage effects may be quite likely to show up below the legislated living wage. In addition, it must be remembered that the centile (10th or otherwise) is only an estimate and may be quite imprecise for smaller cities. Regardless, as explained above, even if workers are pushed above the 10th centile, the estimated average wage of those remaining below the 10th centile will increase.

Nonetheless, to explore the sensitivity of the estimated wage effects for the lowest-wage group to the cutoff used, the specifications were also estimated using the 15th and 20th centiles as cutoffs. To give some perspective on the living wage relative to these centiles, in nine of the cities in Table 1.4, the 15th centile exceeds the living wage, and in six more it is within $1.00 (out of a total of 21 cities). In 14 of the cities, the 20th centile wage exceeds the living wage and is within $1.00 in five more. The estimated 12-month lagged effects for these specifications—corresponding to the estimate of 6.95 in Table 5.3—were 3.62 (standard error of 2.10) using the 15th centile and 3.77 (1.86) using the 20th. Thus, through the 20th centile, the estimated wage effect remains positive and statistically significant at the 5 percent or 10 percent level,

---

[24]As evidence of this, when wage distributions in cities that had implemented living wage laws were closely examined, there was no evidence of spikes at the living wage. A possibility for future research is to adapt non-parametric estimation of wage distributions to identify where in the wage distribution living wage laws induce changes (as is done for the minimum wage and family income distributions in Neumark et al., 1998).

with the point estimate somewhat smaller than that obtained using the 10th centile cutoff, which is not surprising if the effect on lowest-wage workers is greatest.

Assessing the Magnitudes

Returning to Table 5.3, the estimated wage effect for low-wage workers, indicating an elasticity of 0.07 in the lowest decile, is arguably surprisingly large. Since a maximum wage elasticity of 1.0 would be expected for affected workers, the largest effects that should be expected are approximately equal to the proportion of workers who are likely to be affected by the living wage. Using the estimates of this proportion for contractor living wage laws that were reported in Tables 1.1 and 1.3, even assuming that all of the affected workers are in the lowest decile of the wage distribution, the proportion would generally not get very close to 5 percent of the workforce.

To see this, take the coverage estimate to be about 2.5 percent (the approximate 1 percent figure in Tables 1.1 and 1.3, multiplied by 25/10).[25] Next, assume that this 2.5 percent of the workforce gets a raise equal to the living wage increase, which is an exaggeration because this assumes that all of the affected workers were previously at the minimum wage (in the case of a new living wage), rather than above the minimum wage but below the living wage. Under these assumptions, the estimated effect would be only 2.5 (or an elasticity of 0.025), which is less than one-half the size of the estimated effect in the 12-month lag specification in the first column of Table 5.3. Note, also, that an effect of this size would be about equal to the estimated standard error of the corresponding regression coefficient, making it unlikely that an effect on wages from living wage laws that cover and affect only contractors could be detected.[26]

---

[25]To do this calculation, the percentages reported in those tables need to be multiplied by 25/10, since the percentages of affected workers in those tables are based on the assumption that all affected workers are in the lowest quartile, not the lowest decile.

[26]Recall the point raised above that even these low estimates may slightly overstate coverage because living wages are assigned at the level of the metropolitan area rather than the city.

These considerations raise two distinct possibilities that require empirical investigation. First, the baseline estimates may be badly biased, reflecting some influence other than living wages and hence yielding implausibly large estimated effects. Second, the basis for evaluating the plausibility of the estimated living wage effects may be flawed. These issues are discussed below.

Are the Estimates Driven by Covered Workers?

The first approach to the question of whether the estimates truly reflect living wage effects rather than some spurious influence is to estimate separate wage effects for workers more likely and less likely to be covered by living wage ordinances. However, a fundamental difficulty in studying living wage laws using standard household-based datasets is that the researcher does not know which workers are covered by living wage laws. Nonetheless, it is of interest to attempt to identify workers relatively more or less likely to be covered by these laws and to then ask whether wage effects differ between these two groups.

To do this, the limited information available on workers and on the scope of city ordinances is used to try to classify workers as "potentially covered" (or in the "covered sector"). First, attention is limited to the lower quartile of the wage distribution in each city to focus on those more likely to be bound by the living wage law if they are covered. Next, the available information on industries covered by living wage laws is used to estimate the percentage of these workers potentially covered. If the law refers to specific workers (e.g., custodial, security, and parking attendants in Portland, or city employees in a few cities), the same classification is used in the CPS. When the living wage law refers generally to contractors, the workers used are those in construction and in the following service industries: transportation (excluding U.S. Postal workers); communications, utilities, and sanitary services; custodial; protective service; parking; and certain professional and social services. This selection is based on the study of Baltimore's living wage law by Niedt et al. (1999), which looked at the types of workers and firms under city contracts. If the law refers more narrowly to service contractors (e.g.,

San Francisco), construction workers are excluded. Finally, for workers in cities where businesses receiving financial assistance from the city are covered, virtually any nongovernment worker can potentially work for a company that is subject to the legislation. Therefore, all private sector workers in the lowest quartile are characterized as being potentially covered—surely an excessive estimate of actual coverage.

The resulting percentages, based on the CPS data averaged over the 1996–2000 period, are reported in the second column of Table 5.4. Clearly, the estimated percentages should be interpreted as identifying the percentage of workers potentially covered, and hence as providing upper bounds on the percentages of workers actually covered or affected. These upper bounds most likely overstate actual coverage substantially, but the classification may still provide a useful (although noisy) contrast with uncovered workers. By way of contrast, the last columns of Tables 1.1 and 1.3, repeated in the third column of Table 5.4, report estimates of the share of affected workers in the lowest quartile of the wage distribution from reports that have been carried out for some of these cities. As would be expected, given that the latter estimates are intended to measure actual rather than potential coverage, the figures in the third column of Table 5.4 are much lower. This is especially true in the cities with business assistance living wage laws, in part because the city-specific reports generally do not attempt to estimate the percentage of workers affected by business assistance provisions of living wage laws. As will become clear below, the issue of how many workers are covered, or are affected in other ways by living wage laws, is rather central to interpreting the empirical findings. This discussion emphasizes the need to develop data sources that allow researchers to measure labor market outcomes, on the one hand, and to identify workers covered by living wage laws, on the other.

To estimate separate effects of living wages on the wages of potentially covered and uncovered workers, interactions between dummy variables indicating each of these groups of workers (Cov and Uncov) with the living wage variable are added to the specification, to estimate

Table 5.4

Coverage Estimates

City	Coverage Specified in Legislation	Estimated Potential Coverage and Share of Bottom Quartile of Workers in the CPS	External Estimates of Affected Workers and Share of Workers in Bottom Quartile
Baltimore	Construction and service contracts > $5,000	Service industries (18%)	Niedt et al. (1999): 1,494–5,976 (0.51–2.05%)
Boston	Contractors > $100,000; subcontractors > $25,000	Service industries (20%)	
Buffalo	Contractors and subcontractors > $50,000 (> 10 employees)	Service industries (15%)	
Chicago	Contractors and subcontractors	Service industries (18%)	Tolley et al. (1999): 9,807 (1.01%)
Dayton	City employees	City employees (6%)	
Denver	Contractors and subcontractors > $2,000	Service industries (17%)	
Detroit	Contractors, subcontractors, and financial assistance recipients > $50,000	All private sector (90%)	Reynolds (1999): 2,300 (0.40%)
Durham	Contractors, city employees	Service industries plus city employees (25%)	
Hartford	Contractors > $50,000; commercial development projects receiving subsidies > $100,000	All private sector (86%)	
Jersey City	Contractors	Service industries (19%)	
Los Angeles	Service contractors > $25,000; assistance > $100,000 or $1 million lump sum	All private sector (90%)	Pollin and Luce (1998): 7,626 (0.76%)

Table 5.4 (continued)

City	Coverage Specified in Legislation	Estimated Potential Coverage and Share of Bottom Quartile of Workers in the CPS	External Estimates of Affected Workers and Share of Workers in Bottom Quartile
Milwaukee	Contractors and subcontractors > $5,000	Service industries (14%)	
Minneapolis	Assistance > $25,000, as of December 1998; > $100,000 initially	All private sector (91%)	
Oakland	Contractors > $25,000; assistance > $100,000	All private sector (86%)	
Omaha	City employees, contractors > $75,000; assistance > $75,000	All private sector plus city employees (95%)	
Portland	Custodial, security, and parking attendant contracts	Custodial, protective service, parking (3%)	
St. Louis	Contractors and businesses receiving tax breaks	All private sector (90%)	
San Antonio	Businesses receiving tax breaks	All private sector (86%)	
San Francisco	Service contractors > $25,000 ($50,000 for nonprofits); airport leaseholders; home health care workers	Service industries (21%)	Reich et al. (1999): 4,800 (1.99%); Alunan et al. (1999): 4,766 (1.97%)
San Jose	Service contractors > $20,000; assistance > $100,000 (excludes trainees and workers under age 18); city employees	All private sector (excluding workers under age 18), city employees (94%)	Williams (1998): 600 (0.25%)
Tucson	Contractors; assistance > $100,000 annually	All private sector (82%)	

NOTES: The table covers cities with living wages that are included in the wage analysis. The list of service industries includes transportation (excluding U.S. Postal workers), communications, utilities and sanitary services, custodial, protective service, parking, and certain professional and social services. The construction industry is also included when the law refers to contractors generally.

$$\ln(w_{icmy}) = \alpha + X_{icmy}\omega + \beta\ln(w_{cmy}^{min})$$
$$+\gamma\max[\ln(w_{cmy}^{liv}) \times Cov_{icmy}, \ln(w_{cmy}^{min})]$$
$$+\gamma'\max[\ln(w_{cmy}^{liv}) \times Uncov_{icmy}, \ln(w_{cmy}^{liv})] \qquad (5.2)$$
$$+Y_y\delta_Y + M_m\delta_M + C_c\delta_C + \varepsilon_{icmy}.$$

If the estimate of γ indicates positive living wage effects, but the estimate of γ' does not, one should be more confident that the data are detecting actual effects of living wage laws because this would indicate that living wages boost wages only for workers potentially covered by living wage laws.[27]

The estimates of Eq. (5.2) should be interpreted with caution. Some living wage ordinances are not explicit about what types of workers are covered. For many localities, strong assumptions had to be made concerning the types of industries in which covered individuals work. Table 5.4 shows that the broadest definitions of potential coverage were chosen so as not to exclude those who are potentially affected. In addition, at best, those workers who could in principle be covered are identified; actual coverage rates are surely much lower than those reported. Nonetheless, this classification probably distinguishes between workers more and less likely to be covered.

The estimates are reported in Table 5.5. The results indicate that the positive wage effects of living wages show up only for workers who are potentially covered by living wage laws. The estimated effect of living wage laws at a lag of 12 months is statistically significant for covered workers but not for uncovered workers.[28] There is also a statistically

---

[27]Note that when this specification is estimated, the vector X is expanded to include dummy variables representing the worker subgroups that are covered by living wage laws. Since the estimated definition of coverage differs somewhat by city, separate dummy variables for each group are added to pick up wage differences between the groups and to ensure that the interactions are not simply reflecting differences in levels. Also, the interactions with Cov and Uncov appear inside the max operator so that when these variables are zero, the wage floor is specified as the minimum wage, rather than zero.

[28]A Wald test of the equality of coefficients for the 12-month lag specification reveals that the difference in the estimated effects of legislation on covered and uncovered workers is statistically significant.

Table 5.5

Effects of Living Wage Laws on Wages, Potentially Covered and Uncovered Workers

	Uncovered Workers		Covered Workers	
	Centile Range			
	≤ 10	10–25	≤ 10	10–25
Specification 1:	–4.99*	–1.02	2.11	1.23
Living wage	(2.97)	(1.82)	(2.53)	(1.78)
Specification 2:	–4.62	–1.09	5.66**	1.98
Living wage, 6-month lag	(3.07)	(1.92)	(2.56)	(1.89)
Specification 3:	0.61	–1.28	10.61**	2.26
Living wage, 12-month lag	(3.49)	(2.07)	(2.72)	(2.00)
Sample size	34,196	42,638	34,196	42,638

NOTES: See the notes to Tables 5.3 and 5.4. Observations for which allocated information is required to construct the covered and uncovered dummy variables are also dropped.

*Significantly different from zero at the 10 percent level.

**Significantly different from zero at the 5 percent level.

significant positive effect for potentially covered workers in the six-month lag specification. Overall, reiterating the qualification that it is possible to distinguish only crudely between covered and uncovered workers, the results are consistent with those workers more likely to be covered by living wage ordinances receiving the bulk of the wage gains, bolstering the case that the estimated effects of living wage laws are real. Certainly the reverse finding, with stronger wage effects for workers less likely to be covered, would cast doubt on a causal interpretation of the positive overall wage effects reported in Table 5.3.

Are Living Wage Laws Broader Than Is Commonly Thought?

The coverage classification used in the preceding estimates includes all private sector workers in cities where the living wage law covers employers receiving business assistance from the city. Indeed, it is the living wage laws in these cities that drive the wage effects. When those cities are excluded from the sample completely, and Eq. (5.2) is re-estimated, the evidence does not point to statistically significant effects of living wages. This suggests that the wage effects of narrow (contractor only) living wage laws may not be detectable (or may not exist). On the other hand, it emphasizes that many living wage laws are broader than simply mandating higher wages for city contractors (and perhaps city employees). Specifically, when living wage laws extend to employers receiving business assistance, their effective coverage may be more extensive than suggested by the reports summarized in the third column of Table 5.4.[29] This may explain the large living wage effects reported above.[30]

To explore this possibility more directly using all of the data, the basic specification is altered to distinguish between the effects of living wage laws that cover contractors only and those that cover employers receiving business assistance; the latter are surely broader because nearly every living wage law covering business assistance recipients also covers contractors (see Tables 1.1 and 1.3).[31] Dummy variables for the two types of living wage laws (Bus and Con) are interacted with the living wage variable, as in

---

[29]Reynolds (1999) presents crude calculations for Detroit suggesting that taking account of only some employers covered by business assistance provisions more than doubles the number of affected workers. This issue, as well as other reasons why different types of living wage laws may have different effects, requires more serious study in future research.

[30]These may also be enhanced by positive spillover effects from living wages to wages of other workers, for example, as employers grant similar wage increases to their uncovered employees. Whether these spillovers are greater for living wages stemming from business assistance provisions is an open question.

[31]Living wage laws covering city employees only, or city employees and contractors only, are also included in the contractor-only group. However, this concerns only two relatively small cities (Dayton and Durham), and omitting these cities from the analysis had virtually no effect on the estimates.

$$\ln(w_{icmy}) = \alpha + X_{icmy}\omega + \beta \ln(w_{cmy}^{min})$$
$$+ \gamma \max[\ln(w_{cmy}^{liv}) \times Bus_{cmy}, \ln(w_{cmy}^{min})]$$
$$+ \gamma' \max[\ln(w_{cmy}^{liv}) \times Con_{cmy}, \ln(w_{cmy}^{min})] \qquad (5.3)$$
$$+ Y_y \delta_Y + M_m \delta_M + C_c \delta_C + \varepsilon_{icmy}.$$

In this equation, γ' identifies the effect of narrow contractor laws, and γ the effect of living wage laws that extend coverage to employers receiving business assistance. The results, reported in Table 5.6, indicate that the effects of living wage laws on wages are significant only for the cities with the broader laws covering employers receiving business assistance from the city. The estimate is large and statistically significant at a lag of one year and implies an elasticity of 0.11 for workers in the lowest decile. Thus, as the back-of-the-envelope calculation above suggested, there is little evidence of an effect for laws that cover contractors only.

Table 5.6

Effects of Living Wage Laws on Wages, Contractor and Business Assistance Living Wage Laws

	Uncovered Workers		Covered Workers	
	Centile Range			
	≤ 10	10–25	≤ 10	10–25
Specification 1:	–4.50	–2.82	1.78	2.15
Living wage	(3.45)	(2.30)	(2.76)	(2.09)
Specification 2:	–5.22	–2.21	5.83**	2.64
Living wage, 6-month lag	(3.66)	(2.38)	(2.66)	(2.21)
Specification 3:	0.50	–1.92	10.54**	2.72
Living wage, 12-month lag	(4.02)	(2.49)	(2.78)	(2.31)
Sample size	34,435	42,912	34,435	42,912

NOTES: See the notes to Table 5.3.

**Significantly different from zero at the 5 percent level.

Do the Estimated Living Wage Effects Reflect Unmeasured State Policy Changes?

The difference-in-differences strategy used to identify the effects of living wage laws is intended to avoid evidence based on a spurious relationship with other changes in cities passing living wage laws, by using a control sample of cities that did not pass such laws but in which—it is assumed—any of these other changes were similar. An example would be changes in aggregate economic activity that affect low-wage workers similarly in all cities. The fact that there was no evidence of wage effects in higher parts of the wage distribution mitigates concerns about some forms of spurious relationships, in particular those that might be specific to some cities yet have similar effects throughout the wage distribution. Nonetheless, state-level policy changes (or state-level changes in economic conditions) affecting lower-income families may affect labor market outcomes for low-wage workers in particular cities and may coincide with the passage of living wage laws, in which case the estimated effects could still be spurious. Although the specifications did control for state minimum wages, other policies such as state EITCs (Neumark and Wascher, 2001) or welfare reform (Meyer and Rosenbaum, 1999)—some parts of which are not so easily measured—may affect low-wage workers.

To address the possibility that state-level changes exert confounding influences on the estimates of living wage effects, Eq. (5.3) is altered and augmented to use only within-state variation in living wage laws to identify the effect of living wage ordinances on wages. The wage equation now becomes

$$
\begin{aligned}
\ln(w_{icmy}) = {} & \alpha + X_{icmy}\omega + \beta\ln(w_{cmy}^{min}) \\
& + \gamma\max[\ln(w_{cmy}^{liv}) \times Bus_{cmy} \times LW_{cmy}, \ln(w_{cmy}^{min})] \\
& + \gamma'\max[\ln(w_{cmy}^{liv}) \times Con_{cmy} \times LW_{cmy}, \ln(w_{cmy}^{min})] \quad (5.4) \\
& + \theta\max[\ln(w_{cmy}^{liv}), \ln(w_{cmy}^{min})] \\
& + Y_y\delta_Y + M_m\delta_M + C_c\delta_C + \varepsilon_{icmy}.
\end{aligned}
$$

Equation (5.4) embodies two changes. First, the living wage is assigned to all cities in the state.[32] If no city has a living wage, w^{liv} is zero. For all states but California, at most one city in the state has a living wage, in which case all cities in the state get assigned that living wage. In California, where multiple cities have a living wage, a weighted average is used for observations in the state.[33] Second, the living wage variables (still interacted with Bus and Con) are entered directly and interacted with a dummy variable for the city in which the living wage is actually imposed (LW_{cmy}), which is set to one for every month in which the city's living wage law is in effect. This specification allows θ to pick up any state-level changes correlated with living wage changes, whereas γ and γ' capture the differential changes in the city in which the living wage is actually implemented.[34] The latter are the causal effects that this chapter aims to estimate and correspond to what are called "difference-in-difference-in-differences" estimators, using other cities in the same state as another level of controls—this time for state-specific changes.[35] An expanded version of Eq. (5.4) is also estimated where rural workers in the same state are added to the control sample, in which case state dummy variables are also added to the regression. In either case, no longer are the living wage effects inferred from differences in outcomes between all cities that have adopted living wage laws and those that have not. Instead, the effects of living wage laws are identified from the differences in outcomes between cities that have adopted these laws and cities in the same state that have not.

---

[32]For this analysis, individuals in metropolitan areas with living wages that straddle states (Portland and St. Louis) are assumed to be part of the state where the bulk of the metropolitan area residents live (Oregon and Missouri, respectively).

[33]If Oakland, San Francisco, and San Jose are simply dropped, and the Los Angeles living wage is applied to all observations in the state, the results are virtually unaffected.

[34]A specification was also estimated that allowed state-level changes to differ depending on whether the living wage effective in the state was of the business assistance type or the contractor type. This resulted in no appreciable changes in the results.

[35]This limits slightly the number of cities for which an effect can be identified, because Minneapolis and Portland are the only cities in their respective states that are included in our wage sample. For those cities, there is no control group. Thus, for the estimation of the wage effects, the effect of living wages is identified from the remaining cities.

The results are reported in Table 5.7; since wage effects appeared only for the lowest decile of the wage distribution in the previous analysis, attention here is restricted to that decile. The estimated effects on wages are very similar to the corresponding estimates in Table 5.6. Specifically, for living wage laws that apply to employers receiving business assistance, the estimated elasticities of wages with respect to living wages are in the 0.10 to 0.11 range and are statistically significant, whereas the estimated effects for contractor living wage laws are again small and insignificant. This evidence suggests that unmeasured state-level changes correlated with living wage increases do relatively little to bias the estimated effects of living wages.

Does Endogenous Policy Bias the Estimated Living Wage Effects?

The final possibility considered is that city officials time the passage of living wage legislation to coincide with strong economic conditions for

Table 5.7

Effects of Living Wage Laws on Wages, Alternative Control Groups, Bottom Decile

| | Urban Workers in Same State as Control Group | | Urban and Rural Workers in Same State as Control Group | |
| | | Business | | Business |
	Contractor	Assistance	Contractor	Assistance
Specification 1:	−4.36	2.12	−4.17	1.72
Living wage	(3.48)	(3.15)	(3.41)	(3.00)
Specification 2:	−5.40	5.38*	−5.01	5.75*
Living wage, 6-month lag	(3.70)	(3.12)	(3.63)	(2.95)
Specification 3:	0.43	10.39**	0.77	11.27**
Living wage, 12-month lag	(4.08)	(3.32)	(4.00)	(3.12)
Sample size	34,435		51,179	

NOTE: See the notes to Table 5.3.

*Significantly different from zero at the 10 percent level.

**Significantly different from zero at the 5 percent level.

lower-skilled workers, when a living wage is likely to be relatively less binding but will still accomplish whatever political goals might underlie such policies.[36] This sort of timing could provide an alternative explanation of the large estimated wage effects. On the surface, such an explanation seems unlikely to account for much influence on the estimated effects of living wages. As the tables in Chapter 1 indicate, living wages have been implemented in all four regions of the country and are not obviously concentrated in areas with particularly strong economic performance. This is in contrast to, for example, the minimum wage, which is typically set above the federal level mainly in high-wage (Pacific and Northeastern) states. Nonetheless, to attempt to tackle the issue of the timing of the legislation, advantage is taken of the fact that some cities mandated subsequent increases in the living wage at the time they passed their original ordinance. Living wage changes are separated into those that are legislated and those that subsequently result from mandated increases specified earlier. The mandated increases, which are normally part of the original legislation and tie the level of the living wage to federal poverty definitions, are not expected to be as intertwined with economic conditions (at least deliberately) as legislated increases might be.[37]

Estimating these two separate effects requires that Eq. (5.3) include interactions of the living wage effects with indicators for whether the living wage in effect in a particular month is the result of a specific act of legislation (Leg) or was mandated in earlier legislation (Man), as in

---

[36]Although using geographic policy variation to identify and estimate the effects of these policies has a long history in economic research, some recent research has raised questions about this strategy, in at least some contexts. See Besley and Case (2000) and Kubik and Moran (2001).

[37]For every city, the initial living wage is treated as legislated. Subsequent increases are treated as mandated if the living wage is indexed (usually to the poverty line). Thus, in Portland and Baltimore, increases after the initial living wage are treated as legislated, whereas those in other cities are treated as mandated.

$$\ln(w_{icmy}) = \alpha + X_{icmy}\omega + \beta \ln(w_{cmy}^{min})$$

$$+ \gamma \max[\ln(w_{cmy}^{liv}) \times Bus_{cmy} \times Man_{cmy}, \ln(w_{cmy}^{min})]$$

$$+ \gamma' \max[\ln(w_{cmy}^{liv}) \times Con_{cmy} \times Man_{cmy}, \ln(w_{cmy}^{min})]$$

$$+ \delta \max[\ln(w_{cmy}^{liv}) \times Bus_{cmy} \times Leg_{cmy}, \ln(w_{cmy}^{min})]$$

$$+ \delta' \max[\ln(w_{cmy}^{liv}) \times Con_{cmy} \times Leg_{cmy}, \ln(w_{cmy}^{min})]$$

$$+ Y_y \delta_Y + M_m \delta_M + C_c \delta_C + \varepsilon_{icmy}.$$

(5.5)

If the bulk of the positive effect of living wage laws arises from legislated living wage changes, captured in δ (for business assistance living wages), it would be natural to attribute the estimated effects reported above to endogeneity. On the other hand, the effects of mandated increases, captured in γ, should be more immune from bias resulting from the endogenous setting of policy.

Table 5.8 reports the results. As before, positive and statistically significant wage effects are detected only for living wages covering employers receiving business assistance. More to the point, the effects of such living wage laws are considerably stronger for mandated than for legislated increases. For the mandated increases, the evidence now indicates a positive wage effect (with an elasticity of 0.12) that is significant at the 5 percent level in the six-month lag specification. In the 12-month lag specification, the estimated wage effect is positive and statistically significant only for the mandated increases, and the estimate is much larger, with an elasticity of 0.19.[38] These estimates may be implausibly large, suggesting that the results should be interpreted cautiously. Qualitatively, though, because there are, if anything, stronger effects estimated for mandated increases, this evidence contradicts the

---

[38]One potential problem is that mandated increases at a lag of 12 months may largely reflect legislated increases at a lag of 24 months, given that in many cases an initial living wage is passed with mandated increases in subsequent years. To attempt to test for this possibility, lags of 24 months in both legislated and mandated increases were added to the specification, but the estimates tended to be uninformative; given the short period over which living wages have been introduced, this is not surprising.

Table 5.8

Effects of Living Wage Laws on Wages, Legislated and Mandated Increases, Bottom Decile

	Contractor		Business Assistance	
	Legislated	Mandated	Legislated	Mandated
Specification 1:	–2.45	–16.31*	–5.30	7.82**
Living wage	(3.44)	(9.80)	(3.31)	(3.00)
Specification 2:	–5.55	1.78	–1.36	12.17**
Living wage, 6-month lag	(3.89)	(9.20)	(3.36)	(3.06)
Specification 3:	1.89	–5.29	3.98	18.59**
Living wage, 12-month lag	(4.22)	(9.22)	(3.48)	(3.18)

NOTES: See the notes to Table 5.3. The sample size is 34,435.

*Significantly different from zero at the 10 percent level.

**Significantly different from zero at the 5 percent level.

"endogenous timing" hypothesis, under which the positive bias seems most likely to affect the estimates of the effects of legislated increases.[39]

Basic Wage Results for California

As discussed above, the empirical analysis on which this monograph focuses exploits city-level living wage laws across the United States in estimating the effects of these laws to obtain as reliable and precise a set of estimates as possible. Nonetheless, because California is a large state with four large cities that have implemented living wages, it is possible, in principle, to estimate the basic wage equation (5.1) just for California cities, using as a control group California cities identified in the CPS that did not pass living wage laws. Of course, these results must be interpreted cautiously, because the effects of living wage laws using data from California only are identified from the experiences of just four cities, and therefore may not permit enough "averaging" across different types of cities to avoid the influence of idiosyncratic city-specific factors.[40]

---

[39]Alternatively, it suggests that the bias from endogenous policy is in the opposite direction. In any event, the mandated increases provide a more compelling experiment.

[40]For the same reason, attention is restricted to the basic specification because with only four large cities with living wages in California, the effects of different types of living

The results are reported in Table 5.9. Evidence of wage effects is considerably weaker when the sample is restricted to California. In particular, the estimate focused on above—the 12-month lag effect for those in the lowest decile of the wage distribution—is smaller than for the full sample (3.24) and not statistically significant. On the other hand, the sign of the estimated effect is still positive, whereas the estimated 12-month lag effects for higher-wage workers, although also statistically insignificant, are all negative, suggesting a larger relative effect on low-wage workers than is suggested by the 3.24 estimate.[41] This evidence should not be interpreted as implying that living wage laws in California do not raise wages. Rather, the restriction to a small number

Table 5.9

Effects of Living Wage Laws on Wages, Basic Results, California Residents Only

	Centile Range			
	≤ 10	10–25	25–50	50–75
Specification 1:	1.00	5.79	4.08	−1.20
Living wage	(4.24)	(4.94)	(4.58)	(4.26)
Specification 2:	−2.31	−2.98	−1.21	−2.28
Living wage, 6-month lag	(4.32)	(4.90)	(4.79)	(4.60)
Specification 3:	3.24	−2.09	−4.06	−3.75
Living wage, 12-month lag	(4.25)	(4.82)	(4.96)	(4.71)
Sample size	4,504	5,027	8,792	8,928

NOTES: See the notes to Table 5.3. A total of 11 metropolitan areas are used in the analysis, including Bakersfield, Fresno, Los Angeles-Long Beach, Oakland, Orange County, Riverside-San Bernardino, Sacramento, San Diego, San Francisco, San Jose, and Vallejo-Fairfield-Napa.

---

wage laws cannot be reliably estimated. For example, only San Francisco excludes employers receiving business assistance, so the differential effect of this type of living wage law would be identified solely from differences relative to San Francisco.

[41]Thus, the difference-in-difference-in-differences estimate for the lowest-wage workers, which is the difference between the estimate for these workers and that for higher-wage workers, is in the 5.3 to 7 range, not very different from the corresponding estimate in Table 5.3 of 6.95.

of living wage cities and control cities renders the estimates largely uninformative. Focusing again on the 12-month lag effect for the lowest-wage workers, the standard error in Table 5.9 is 4.25, compared with 2.40 in Table 5.3. Absent a compelling reason to believe that the estimates for the United States as a whole do not apply to California, and absent any strong indication that the results for California are greatly different from those for the United States as a whole, it appears that the latter estimates should be taken as providing reasonably reliable evidence on the effects of living wages in California.

Conclusions

Using standard household-level labor market data, the evidence points to sizable effects of living wage ordinances on the wages of low-wage workers in the cities in which these ordinances are enacted. Aside from providing estimates of the effects of living wage laws that have been implemented to date in cities across the United States, and demonstrating that living wage laws are effective, the empirical evidence regarding the positive effects of living wage laws on the wages of low-wage workers indicates that there is a potentially fruitful research agenda on the effects of these laws that can be pursued exploiting cross-city variation in household-level datasets (although other research designs and data collection strategies should also be explored). More specifically, this evidence argues for a detailed analysis of the CPS data to assess whether living wage ordinances ultimately achieve their policy goal of helping poor or low-income families. Such an analysis is provided in subsequent chapters.

Turning to a more detailed summary of the substantive results, the magnitudes of the estimated wage effects are much larger than would be expected given the apparently limited coverage of city contractors by living wage laws. Additional analyses of these wage effects indicate that the large effects do not appear to be driven by spurious or endogenous relationships stemming from other state-level policy changes or the timing of policy changes to coincide with advantageous economic conditions. Rather, the effects are driven by cities in which the coverage of living wage laws is more broad—namely, cities that impose living wages on employers receiving business assistance from the city.[42]

This leads to three points that should influence one's reading of some past research on living wages and shape future research. First, existing analyses of the likely effects of living wage laws based on narrow coverage and ignoring business assistance provisions may be quite misleading.

Second, at least some living wage ordinances—specifically those with business assistance provisions—may operate somewhat more like relatively broad minimum wage laws than like narrow living wage laws centered on city contractors and city employees. Although this suggests that conclusions from the minimum wage literature may be somewhat informative about the effects of living wage laws, living wage laws are nonetheless sufficiently different—aside from their much higher mandated wage floors—that independent evaluation of their success in helping low-wage workers and poor families is warranted.

Third, even though positive wage effects appear to stem from those cities with broader (i.e., business assistance) living wage laws, the magnitudes of the effects may still appear to some as implausibly large, and much more study is needed to assess the magnitudes of wage effects that might be expected. At this point, unfortunately, there is not enough information to fully evaluate this question. Some research suggests that,

---

[42]Bertrand et al. (2001) examine the effect of serial correlation in the error term (and the data) across observations on the same unit (in this case, cities) on standard difference-in-differences estimators. They find that, especially in the absence of statistical diagnostic tests, these estimators are likely to lead to biased and often understated standard errors and hence erroneous findings of statistical significance. Kezdi (2001) shows that unbiased estimates of the standard errors allowing an arbitrary serial correlation pattern in the error can be obtained easily, by "clustering" the data by city (rather than by city and month). However, the resulting standard errors are conservative (if anything too large), because no structure is imposed on the serial correlation. This estimator was implemented for all the key specifications underlying the conclusions in this monograph. Although the standard errors generally rose somewhat, the changes were not dramatic. The results for the business assistance living wage laws—which are the types of laws for which significant effects are found throughout this monograph— remained statistically significant at the 5 or 10 percent level. And most of the results based on specifications that did not distinguish between types of living wage laws remained statistically significant at the 5 or 10 percent level (the only exception being some of the results for poverty).

at least in the early going, compliance with living wage laws in one city (Los Angeles) was not strongly enforced (Sander and Lokey, 1998). More study of compliance would help to assess the reliability of estimated wage effects such as those reported in this chapter. Similarly, there is little information on coverage by business assistance living wage laws; clearly, the greater this coverage, the more plausible the larger estimates of wage effects will be. Finally, understanding the potential channels of living wage effects—direct effects on contractors, direct effects on those covered by business assistance laws, spillovers to other employees of covered employers as well as to other employers, etc.—will be essential to better understanding how living wage laws influence wages and therefore other labor market outcomes.

6. What Are the Employment Effects of Living Wage Laws?

The previous chapter was concerned with establishing whether it is possible to detect effects of living wages on the outcome that should be affected most directly, namely, wages. That chapter established that there appears to be a detectable, causal effect of broader living wage laws that cover employers receiving business assistance from the city. Higher wages are clearly one goal of living wage laws. But the potential gains from higher wages may be offset by reduced employment opportunities. To examine such a tradeoff, this study now turns briefly to a parallel analysis of the employment effects of living wage laws.

Evidence of Employment Effects

The framework used to estimate employment effects of living wage laws is the same as that used to study the effects of these laws on wages.[1] In particular, the same specifications are used as in the analysis of wages, substituting individual employment status as the dependent variable and using linear probability models, which measure the effect of living wages on the probability of employment. The only difference is that nonworking individuals cannot be classified based on their position in the wage distribution. Instead, wages are imputed for everyone, and the imputed wage distribution is used to classify individuals based on predicted wages.[2]

---

[1]There was no statistically significant evidence of effects on hours worked, so only employment results are reported.

[2]The regression used to predict wages included controls for education, age (up to a cubic), race, gender, marital status, number of family members, number of children under age 18, year, and interview month. If actual wages for workers and imputed wages for nonworkers were used, there would rarely be nonworkers in the extreme percentiles of the wage distribution.

Graphical Analysis

As for wages, it is useful to examine graphical displays of the data before turning to the regression results. Displays paralleling those for wages, but focusing on the employment of those in the lowest decile of the predicted wage distribution, are presented in Figures 6.1 and 6.2. Figure 6.1 displays the data for the largest cities, those with at least 25 observations per month in every month of the sample.[3] These figures more commonly reveal employment declines (in nine of the 17 cities displayed versus six revealing employment increases).

Figure 6.2 presents the event analysis. The changes are not sharp (which is also reflected in the subsequent regression analysis). However, the graph does suggest that the living wage cities had higher employment rates prior to the passage of living wage laws, whereas employment rates in these cities dropped in relative terms with the passage of living wage laws, and especially with a longer lag.

Regression Results

The basic results with no distinction as to the type of living wage law or more refined attempts to address causality are reported in Table 6.1. Above the 10th centile, there is no evidence of disemployment effects, which is not surprising given the lack of wage effects. Interestingly, there is evidence of positive employment effects between the 50th and 75th centiles, consistent with substitution toward higher-skilled workers (as discussed in Chapter 2). However, focusing attention on those at the

---

The market wages faced by those who choose not to work may be lower than those faced by observationally equivalent individuals who choose to work; this is the standard sample selection problem (Heckman, 1979). To assess the consequences of this in a simple manner, the estimates were recalculated reducing the predicted wages of the nonworkers by 5 percent and 10 percent. The results reported below were qualitatively similar.

For the employment estimates, the effect is identified for three additional cities with living wage laws (Duluth, Madison, and New Haven), because with the inclusion of nonworkers these cities have 25 or more observations for some months both before and after the implementation of a living wage; in general, there are many more city-month cells with 25 or more observations when looking at employment.

[3] As just noted, there are more of these cities for the employment analysis because nonworkers are included.

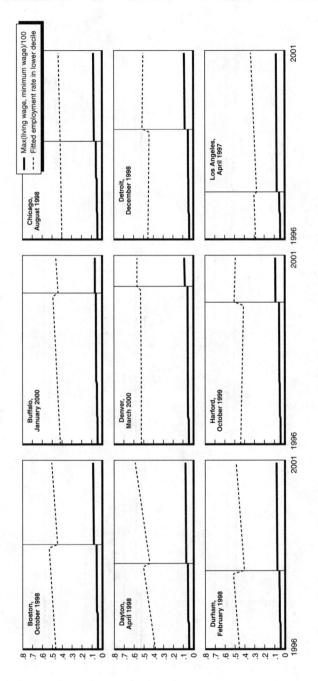

Figure 6.1—Employment

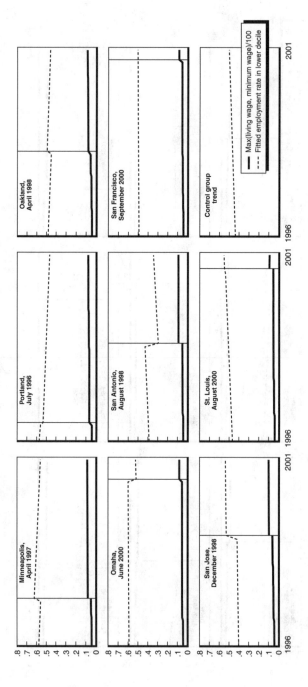

Figure 6.1 (continued)

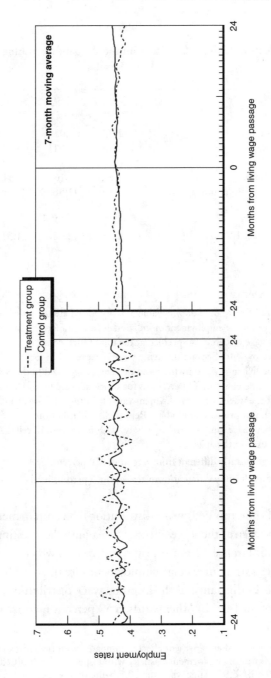

Figure 6.2—Event Analysis, Employment

Table 6.1

Effects of Living Wage Laws on the Probability of Employment, Basic Results

	Centile Range			
	≤ 10	10–25	25–50	50–75
Specification 1:	−1.77	0.02	2.58**	1.79*
Living wage	(2.14)	(1.81)	(1.18)	(1.04)
Specification 2:	−3.22	1.16	2.31*	1.32
Living wage, 6-month lag	(2.26)	(1.88)	(1.24)	(1.08)
Specification 3:	−5.62**	1.62	1.55	2.44**
Living wage, 12-month lag	(2.45)	(2.02)	(1.31)	(1.16)
Sample size	83,326	118,541	197,477	199,703
Mean percentage employed	43.98	58.70	68.80	79.12

NOTES: See the notes to Table 5.3. Reported are the estimated effects of the living wage on the employment of individuals in the range of a metropolitan area's imputed wage distribution specified at the top of each column. All estimates are multiplied by 100. Because the living wage is expressed in logs, elasticities are given by the coefficient divided by the mean percentage reported in the last row of the corresponding column. Observations for which allocated information is required to construct the wage or the employment variable in the CPS are dropped. Estimates are from linear probability models. Reported standard errors are robust to nonindependence (and heteroscedasticity) within city-month cells. A total of 223 cities are used in the analyses.

*Significantly different from zero at the 10 percent level.
**Significantly different from zero at the 5 percent level.

bottom of the (imputed) wage distribution, the employment effects mirror (in reverse) the wage effects, with a fairly large estimated negative effect (−5.62) in the 12-month lag specification, which is statistically significant. Given an average employment rate of about 0.4 for individuals in this range of the imputed wage distribution, this implies an elasticity of −0.14.[4] In other words, a 50 percent increase in the living

---

[4]If the estimated employment effect is compared with the estimated wage effect, the evidence indicates an employment elasticity with respect to the "realized" wage increase of −2 ({−5.62/0.40}/−6.95), larger than the −0.5 figure that is taken as a consensus in the

wage would reduce the employment rate for this group by 7 percent, or 2.8 percentage points.[5]

Looking next at the distinction between contractor-only living wage laws and business assistance laws in Table 6.2, the results partly mirror the wage effects. In particular, in the 12-month lag specification for the lowest-skilled individuals, only for living wage laws with business assistance provisions is the estimated disemployment effect (–5.88)

Table 6.2

Effects of Living Wage Laws on the Probability of Employment, Contractor vs. Business Assistance Living Wage Laws

	Contractor Living Wage		Business Assistance Living Wage	
	Centile Range			
	≤ 10	10–25	≤ 10	10–25
Specification 1:	–3.26	0.59	–0.81	–0.34
Living wage	(3.19)	(2.75)	(2.73)	(2.26)
Specification 2:	–5.49	1.03	–1.74	1.24
Living wage, 6-month lag	(3.40)	(2.85)	(2.90)	(2.36)
Specification 3:	–5.26	1.45	–5.88*	1.74
Living wage, 12-month lag	(3.79)	(3.06)	(3.06)	(2.54)
Sample size	83,326	118,541	83,326	118,541

NOTE: See the notes to Table 6.1.

*Significantly different from zero at the 10 percent level.

labor demand literature (Hamermesh, 1993). This suggests that the estimated disemployment effect, insofar as it arises solely because of the "average" wage effect of living wages, is larger than would be expected. However, living wages may entail greater increases in projected future labor costs than the wage increase that identifies the typical labor demand elasticity, given the frequent indexation of living wages. Also, this elasticity focuses on one narrow category of workers, rather than labor overall, so that substitution possibilities may be greater.

[5]As noted in Chapter 5, this analysis was repeated allowing for different trends for the cities that passed living wage laws in the sample period and those that did not. This had no qualitative effect upon the conclusions. As with the wage results, the conclusions were the same in specifications adding the contemporaneous or six-month lags of the minimum variable.

statistically significant (at the 10 percent level); this corresponds exactly to the specification and type of living wage laws for which the evidence indicated that living wage laws boost wages. In contrast, although the point estimate of the employment effect for contractor-only living wage laws is not as different in magnitude as was the estimated wage effect, it is not significantly different from zero.

Tables 6.3 and 6.4 also parallel the previous analysis of wage effects by conducting the two experiments meant to assess the causality question, first using urban or urban and rural workers in the same state as the control group, and then distinguishing between mandated and legislated increases, looking only at individuals below the 10th centile of the imputed wage distribution. Again mirroring the wage results, the estimated disemployment effects are relatively insensitive to the alternative control groups considered, although the estimates are less

Table 6.3

Effects of Living Wage Laws on the Probability of Employment,
Alternative Control Groups, Bottom Decile

	Urban Workers in Same State as Control Group		Urban and Rural Workers in Same State as Control Group	
	Contractor	Business Assistance	Contractor	Business Assistance
Specification 1:	−2.93	−0.05	−3.43	0.69
Living wage	(3.23)	(2.97)	(3.14)	(2.85)
Specification 2:	−5.31	−1.33	−5.53*	−0.65
Living wage, 6-month lag	(3.43)	(3.16)	(3.33)	(3.02)
Specification 3:	−4.93	−5.21	−5.21	−4.43
Living wage, 12-month lag	(3.82)	(3.34)	(3.75)	(3.20)
Sample size	83,326		118,355	

NOTE: See the notes to Table 6.1.

*Significantly different from zero at the 10 percent level.

Table 6.4

Effects of Living Wage Laws on the Probability of Employment,
Legislated vs. Mandated Increases, Bottom Decile

	Contractor		Business Assistance	
	Legislated	Mandated	Legislated	Mandated
Specification 1:	–0.97	–16.15**	–2.86	0.74
Living wage	(3.25)	(7.39)	(3.20)	(3.35)
Specification 2:	–4.17	–12.23*	–1.98	–1.62
Living wage, 6-month lag	(3.67)	(6.93)	(3.43)	(3.71)
Specification 3:	–4.20	–11.02	–5.52	–6.29
Living wage, 12-month lag	(4.10)	(6.98)	(3.88)	(3.95)

NOTES: See the notes to Table 6.1. The sample size is 83,326.

*Significantly different from zero at the 10 percent level.

**Significantly different from zero at the 5 percent level.

precise.[6] Similarly, the estimated disemployment effects are considerably larger for mandated living wage increases, although the estimates are not statistically significant at the 10 percent level. Curiously, the evidence for mandated living wage increases points to larger effects of contractor-only laws. But the estimate for the 12-month lag is quite imprecise, and the other estimated effects appear implausibly large. This raises some questions about the ability of the data to support the more disaggregated analysis by legislated and mandated increases in the case of employment effects.

Results for California

Again, the basic specification can be estimated using data for California cities only (see Table 6.5). As with the wage results, the estimates for California only are considerably less precise. Roughly speaking, though, the estimates look similar, with the largest negative effect (although only marginally significant) for the lowest-skilled

---

[6]The additional cities with living wages that enter the sample (Duluth, Madison, and New Haven) are in states with other (larger) cities that have living wages. Thus, as described above following Eq. (5.4) for the analysis of wages, a weighted average of living wages in the state is used for the other workers in the state used as the control group.

Table 6.5

Effects of Living Wage Laws on the Probability of Employment, Basic Results, California Residents Only

	Centile Range			
	≤ 10	10–25	25–50	50–75
Specification 1:	−2.63	−7.33	5.79**	7.09**
Living wage	(5.86)	(4.76)	(2.75)	(2.94)
Specification 2:	−3.83	0.73	1.90	5.13*
Living wage, 6-month lag	(6.04)	(4.85)	(2.96)	(3.10)
Specification 3:	−9.18	1.34	3.37	4.25
Living wage, 12-month lag	(6.07)	(4.91)	(3.08)	(3.33)
Sample size	9,652	13,942	23,224	23,392
Mean percentage employed	36.38	58.96	66.78	75.64

NOTES: See the notes to Table 6.1. A total of 21 metropolitan areas are used in the analysis. In addition to those listed in Table 5.9, these include Chico-Paradise, Merced, Modesto, San Luis Obispo-Atascadero-Paso Robles, Santa Barbara-Santa Maria-Lompoc, Santa Rosa, Stockton-Lodi, Ventura, Visalia-Tulare-Porterville, and Yuba City.

*Significantly different from zero at the 10 percent level.

**Significantly different from zero at the 5 percent level.

individuals in the 12-month lag specification. Again, there is little indication that the results for the United States as a whole do not provide a reliable indication of the effects of living wage laws in California cities.

Conclusions

The evidence on employment effects is weaker than the evidence on wage effects. The point estimates indicating disemployment effects are less often statistically significant, especially in the disaggregated analyses meant to provide more stringent tests of a causal interpretation of the results. But the negative employment effects tend to appear in the same specifications and subsamples for which the positive wage effects appear. Overall, then, the combined evidence is more consistent with the view that the positive wage effects of living wage laws—in particular the broader laws that apply to employers receiving business assistance—are accompanied by disemployment effects among the potentially affected workers, pointing to tradeoffs between wages and employment. This is what economic theory would lead us to expect and sets the stage for the next chapter, where these (and other) competing effects are weighed in examining the effect of living wage laws on urban poverty.

7. Do Living Wage Ordinances Reduce Urban Poverty?

Living wage laws are pitched by advocates as antipoverty programs. For example, the National Living Wage Resource Center, a website maintained by the Association of Community Organizations for Reform Now (ACORN), a leading force behind the living wage movement, states that "Our limited public dollars should not be subsidizing poverty-wage work," noting that in such cases "tax payers end up footing a double bill: the initial subsidy and then the food stamps, emergency medical, housing and other social services low wage workers may require to support themselves and their families even minimally."[1] The Economic Policy Institute, although noting that other antipoverty tools are needed, argues that "the living wage is a crucial tool in the effort to end poverty."[2] And Pollin and Luce argue that "[T]he basic premise of the living movement is simple: that anyone in this country who works for a living should not have to raise a family in poverty" (1998, p. 1). Reflecting this antipoverty goal, existing living wage ordinances often mandate that covered employers must pay their workers a wage sufficient to lift a family above the poverty level. For example, the Detroit living wage is set to 100 percent of the poverty line for a family of four if health benefits are paid, and 125 percent without health benefits.

To this point, this monograph has documented the positive effect of living wages on the wages of low-wage workers, and has provided some evidence of offsetting negative employment effects for low-skilled individuals. These offsetting effects imply that—as economic theory would predict—there are both winners and losers from living wage

---

[1] See www.livingwagecampaign.org.

[2] See www.epinet.org/Issueguides/livingwage/livingwagefaq.html.

laws.[3] As pointed out above, the situation is even more complicated when trying to ask whether living wage laws help low-income families, because many low-wage workers are not in poor or even low-income families and because the preceding estimates tell us nothing about the distribution of the wage and employment effects across families with different incomes.

The analysis in this chapter tries to assess whether living wage laws help to reduce urban poverty. The empirical strategy is to ask whether the probability that a family is poor declines in cities implementing living wage laws, and more so when living wages are higher, compared to a control sample of cities that do not pass living wage laws. In a sense, this analysis treats the effects of living wage laws as a "black box," estimating their overall effect without fully disentangling the relationships between living wages, their effects on low-wage workers and low-skilled individuals, and the distribution of these effects across families. Although these more complicated relationships are of interest, the analysis presented in this chapter is a crucial first step in trying to establish the net effect of living wage laws. Data do not currently permit a full disentangling of the underlying relationships.

A finding that living wage laws reduce poverty would not necessarily imply that these laws increase economic welfare overall (or vice versa). Surely someone pays for the higher wages induced by living wage laws, and interpersonal comparisons leading to overall welfare calculations are notoriously problematic (see Sen, 1997). In addition, living wage laws, like all tax and transfer schemes, generally entail some inefficiencies that may reduce welfare relative to the most efficient such scheme. However, it seems clear that policymakers and the public regard the poverty rate as an important metric and living wages as a viable means of attempting to reduce it. Thus, the effect of living wage laws on urban poverty is an important policy issue. If living wage laws fail to reduce urban poverty, the principal argument of living wage advocates would be undermined. But if they achieve this goal, considerations of potential costs of living

---

[3]Recall also that the estimated positive wage effects could in principle arise from disemployment effects. An explicit analysis of the effects of living wages on income, without conditioning on employment status, avoids this ambiguity in assessing whether the evidence points to gains or losses.

wages and comparisons with other possible alternatives would become quite important.

Data

The data were discussed extensively in Chapter 5. However, the primary analysis in this chapter uses the CPS ADF files from 1996 through 2000. As explained above, these are the most appropriate files for studying family earnings or income. However, one initial analysis that ties the estimation of poverty effects most closely to the analysis of wage and employment effects in the previous chapters, described below, continues to use the ORGs.

Effects on Poverty-Level Earnings

As suggested above, living wage laws are designed to enable a person to earn enough to lift his or her family out of poverty. The first analysis describes evidence on whether living wage ordinances are likely to achieve this goal. Two types of hypothetical families are considered: families with one parent and two children, and families with two parents and two children. For this analysis, the ORG data are used.[4] The analysis focuses on whether an individual's earnings (assuming a full year of work) are below the poverty line for each of these two types of families, defining variables P^1 and P^2 that are, respectively, dummy variables denoting whether a worker's earnings would place him or her below the poverty line for one- and two-parent, two-child families.[5] Regressions are estimated of the form

$$P_{icmy}^k = \alpha + \beta \ln(w_{cmy}^{min}) + \gamma \max[\ln(w_{cmy}^{liv}), \ln(w_{cmy}^{min})]$$
$$+ Y_y \delta_Y + M_m \delta_M + C_c \delta_C + \varepsilon_{icmy}, k = 1, 2. \qquad (7.1)$$

In this regression, estimates of γ that are less than zero indicate that living wages increase the probability that an individual's earnings would

---

[4]Recall the warning in Chapter 5 about the definition of poverty at a monthly frequency.

[5]Following Census Bureau recommendations, the CPI is used to inflate 1999 poverty lines for 2000.

be sufficient to lift his or her family out of poverty. What this regression asks, essentially, is whether changes in wages induced by living wages push earnings over particular thresholds relevant to the policy debate. This is not necessarily the most meaningful analysis of the effects of living wages on poverty, among other reasons because it does not use information on the actual family structure—which determines the poverty line. But it does parallel the calculations used by advocates of living wages. Here, employment effects are ignored, because the calculations are done only for those with a wage, and effects on hours worked are ignored, except for hours variation across nonhourly workers.

Estimates of Eq. (7.1) are reported in Table 7.1. There are no significant effects of living wages in providing earnings sufficient to lift families out of poverty, whether on the basis of one- or two-parent families. In contrast, there is evidence from the specifications with contemporaneous effects or six-month lags that minimum wage increases could accomplish this goal for families with a single parent and two children, with the effects significant at the 10 percent level. However, a year after the minimum wage increase, the estimated effects are no longer significant, consistent with the dissipation of wage effects reported earlier.[6]

Of course, these estimates relate to "hypothetical" families. Different answers are possible in looking at actual families and at the earnings of all family members. In addition, these estimates ignore employment effects, because they apply to workers only. Finally, these estimates do not incorporate the effects of living wage ordinances on hours worked. The analysis therefore next turns to overall or net effects on poverty that take account of all of these factors.

Effects of Living Wages on Poverty

Two related questions are considered. First, as just noted, living wage laws are designed to help families escape poverty. Thus, the first question considered is whether living wage laws increase the probability that families' earnings exceed the poverty line. For the earnings analysis,

---

[6]The results were nearly identical using as dependent variables the percentage of families in the city-month cell below the poverty line, based on this earnings measure.

Table 7.1

Contemporaneous and Lagged Effects on the Probability That a Worker's Earnings Are Below Particular Poverty Lines

	Assumed Family Size	
	Single Parent, 2 Children	2 Parents, 2 Children
Specification 1:		
Minimum wage	–4.14*	0.35
	(2.44)	(2.71)
Living wage	1.09	0.99
	(0.79)	(0.88)
Specification 2:		
Minimum wage, 6-month lag	–4.76*	–0.03
	(2.51)	(2.76)
Living wage, 6-month lag	0.58	0.80
	(0.82)	(0.92)
Specification 3:		
Minimum wage, 12-month lag	–2.06	1.66
	(2.56)	(2.77)
Living wage, 12-month lag	–0.28	0.66
	(0.87)	(0.97)
Mean percentage below poverty	28.14	19.32

NOTES: See the notes to Table 5.3. Reported are the estimated effects of minimum wages and living wages effective in a metropolitan area on the probability that a worker's earnings are below the specified poverty line, if each wage earner was the only source of income in a family, using linear probability models. All estimates are multiplied by 100. Because the living wage is expressed in logs, elasticities are given by the coefficient divided by the mean percentage reported in the last row of the corresponding column. Poverty thresholds are imputed for 2000 using the CPI. Estimates are from linear probability models. Reported standard errors are robust to nonindependence (and heteroscedasticity) within city-month cells. The sample size is 283,037.

*Significantly different from zero at the 10 percent level.

an annual family earnings measure is constructed by summing individual annual earnings of the members of the family. Note that the resulting definition of poverty does not correspond to the "official" definition, because only data on earnings are used and not data on total family income, including unearned income, transfers, etc.[7] Nonetheless, the effect of living wages on the ability of families to earn their way out of poverty is an important policy question, as policies that accomplish such goals via earnings rather than transfers tend to attract more political support (e.g., the EITC vs. AFDC).

Following the earnings analysis, a parallel analysis using total family income is carried out. If fighting poverty is the goal of living wages, these estimates are perhaps more appropriate than the estimates obtained using just total family earnings. Not only do they take into account both the gains in family earnings that result from living wages if wages of family members increase, and the declines in family earnings that result if employment or hours are reduced as a result of the legislation, but they also take into account changes in transfer income or other income received as a result of the changing wages, hours, or employment status of family members.

In both cases, whether a family's earnings or income is below the poverty line (denoted by P) is computed, and the following equation estimated:

$$P_{icmy} = \alpha + \beta \ln(w_{cmy}^{min}) + \gamma \max[\ln(w_{cmy}^{liv}), \ln(w_{cmy}^{min})]$$
$$+ Y_y \delta_Y + M_m \delta_M + C_c \delta_C + \varepsilon_{icmy}.$$

(7.2)

As explained above, this analysis uses the March ADFs, which contain information on family earnings and income.[8] However, because

---

[7]In this analysis, families with members age 65 or older are excluded. Because of Social Security, those who are at least age 65 are more likely to have substantially greater income than earnings.

Another issue this raises is that of before-tax and after-tax income. Although using the CPS income measure instead of earnings accounts for some changes in transfers induced by changes in earnings, it does not account for changes in taxes (or the EITC). For a detailed discussion of marginal tax rates on low-income workers—suggesting that these tax rates are often quite high—see Shaviro (1999).

[8]The equations are estimated for families currently residing in the city. Thus, it is possible, in principle, that in- or out-migration of families in response to living wage laws affects the probability that families living in a particular city are poor. However, it seems unlikely that this could have more than a negligible effect.

the ADFs cover all individuals in the sample in March, rather than one-fourth (as in the ORGs), there is a much larger set of metropolitan areas for which there are at least 25 observations.

Graphical Analysis

Again, a graphical representation of the data is useful. In this case, only annual data are available, so the graphs based on city-specific regressions (paralleling Figures 5.1 and 6.1) are not informative. However, Figure 7.1 depicts the event analysis (paralleling Figures 5.2 and 6.2); with annual data, smoothing is not necessary. The top two graphs in Figure 7.1 display the event analysis for poverty based on earnings (left) and income (right). Although the graphs extend from four years before to four years following living wage increases, there are very few observations either three or more years before or two or more years after a living wage increase. This is depicted in the bottom two graphs, which display the same lines, but with the plotting points for the treatment group (the circles) proportional in area to the number of cities on which the points are based. These circles are very small for the points at –4 and at 3 or 4, and rather small at –3 and 2, relative to the other circles.[9] Thus, attention should focus to some extent on the period from two years before to one year after the implementation of living wage laws. The graphs over these periods give some indication of declines in poverty associated with living wage increases, looking at either earnings or income.

Regression Results

The regression analysis begins by using the 1997–2000 ADFs, which contain information on family earnings and income from 1996–1999. This corresponds as closely as possible to the years covered by the ORG data.[10] Estimates of Eq. (7.2) are reported in Table 7.2. Looking at earnings, the first column presents the estimates of the effects of living

---

[9]In particular, the numbers of cities at each point in the graph (in parentheses) were: 3 (–4), 8 (–3), 15 (–2), 17 (–1), 19 (0), 16 (1), 8 (2), 4 (3), and 2 (4).

[10]The 2001 ADF covering 2000 was not available when this research was conducted. It was confirmed, though, that using the ORG data through 1999 yields the same wage and employment effects as reported in Tables 5.3 and 6.1.

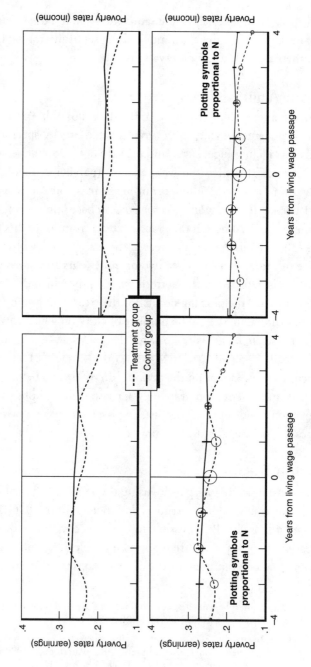

Figure 7.1—Event Analysis, Poverty

Table 7.2

Contemporaneous and Lagged Effects on the Probability That Family Earnings or Income Falls Below the Poverty Line

	Effects on the Probability That Families Have Total Earnings Below the Poverty Line		Effects on the Probability That Families Have Total Income Below the Poverty Line	
Specification 1:				
Minimum wage (December)	−7.29	−2.18	−13.77*	−9.09*
	(6.27)	(4.84)	(7.08)	(5.44)
Living wage (December)	−3.27**	−2.20*	−0.61	−0.03
	(1.45)	(1.31)	(1.60)	(1.46)
Specification 2:				
Minimum wage, 6-month lag	−1.03	3.44	−8.39	−3.30
(June)	(5.83)	(4.82)	(6.63)	(5.51)
Living wage, 6-month lag (June)	−4.73**	−4.26**	−1.46	−1.32
	(1.61)	(1.41)	(1.79)	(1.67)
Specification 3:				
Minimum wage, 12-month lag	−5.54	−2.07	−3.54	−0.28
(January)	(5.33)	(4.78)	(6.58)	(5.86)
Living wage, 12-month lag	−5.08**	−4.84**	−3.85**	−3.34*
(January)	(1.44)	(1.35)	(1.76)	(1.73)
Dataset	ADF	ADF	ADF	ADF
Sample restrictions	≥ 25 per cell	≥ 25 per cell	≥ 25 per cell	≥ 25 per cell
Years that sample covers	96–99	95–99	96–99	95–99
Number of observations	107,821	134,584	82,195	103,601
Mean percentage below poverty	25.78	26.01	18.62	18.73

NOTES: Reported are the estimated effects of minimum wages and living wages effective in a metropolitan area on whether a family's earnings or income are below poverty, using linear probability models. All estimates are multiplied by 100. Because the living wage is expressed in logs, elasticities are given by the coefficient divided by the mean percentage reported in the last row of the corresponding column. Given that the ADF surveys are conducted in March and information on family earnings and income refers to the prior calendar year, the applicable contemporaneous and lagged minimum and living wages are noted in parentheses in the specification descriptions. The ADF regressions include year dummy variables instead of month dummy variables. Observations for which allocated information is required to construct the total earnings variable or the total income variable in the CPS are dropped for the relevant analyses. Reported standard errors are robust to non-independence (and heteroscedasticity) within city-month cells. A total of 229 cities are used in the earnings analyses and 218 in the income analysis.

*Significantly different from zero at the 10 percent level.

**Significantly different from zero at the 5 percent level.

wages (and minimum wages) on poverty.[11] The estimated living wage effects are consistent with living wages reducing poverty, as the estimates for the contemporaneous, six-month, and 12-month lag specifications are negative and significant. The estimates are stronger the longer the lag, consistent with the pattern of estimated wage effects (although the negative employment effects also strengthened with the lag length). In the second column we use the larger sample, adding data from 1995 (for which identifying SMSAs in the ADF is not problematic, unlike the ORGs). This results in the estimated coefficients falling in absolute value, while remaining negative and generally significant.

The third and fourth columns turn to the analysis of living wage legislation and poverty based on total family income. In both columns, the estimated effects of living wages on the probability that a family is poor are always negative, but statistically significant (at the 5 percent or 10 percent level) only in the 12-month lag specification. The estimates for the effects of living wages using total income to classify families as poor indicate that a 10 percent increase in the living wage reduces the probability that a family lives in poverty by 0.0033 to 0.0039. Given that 19 percent of families have income below the poverty level (last row of Table 7.2), the implied elasticity is about –0.19.[12]

It is worth considering whether the estimated effects on poverty are plausible, given the magnitudes of the wage effects noted above indicating that a similar 10 percent increase in the living wage boosts the

---

[11]Since the ADFs contain earnings and income information from the prior calendar year, the estimated effects of the December living wage, the June living wage, and the January living wage correspond roughly to the effects of the contemporaneous living wage, the living wage lagged six months, and the living wage lagged 12 months in the ORGs, respectively. The same is true of minimum wages. Estimates were also obtained using a weighted average of the applicable minimum and living wage in the metropolitan area over the year. As might be expected, the estimated effects were quite close to the estimated effects using the June (i.e., mid-year) minimum wage and living wage.

[12]Again, this analysis was repeated allowing for different trends for the cities that passed living wage laws in the sample period and those that did not. This had no qualitative effect on the conclusions. The analysis was also done using as the control group only non-living wage cities in the same states as cities passing living wage laws, as was done for wages in Chapter 5; again the results were unaffected. Finally, as for the wage results, the conclusions were the same in specifications adding the contemporaneous minimum wage variable or the six-month lag.

average wages of low-wage workers by only 0.7 percentage point. Of course, no one is claiming that living wages lift a family from well below the poverty line to well above it. But living wages may help nudge some families over the poverty line, especially when we recognize that this estimated wage impact is an average effect, whereas the more likely scenario is larger gains concentrated on fewer workers and families. For example, if the 0.7 percentage point average wage increase is concentrated on 10 percent of low-wage workers (1 percent of workers overall), then the implied wage increase for them is 7 percent. If we consider a worker earning the federal minimum, this translates into an earnings increase of $720 over the course of the year for a full-time worker; for a higher-wage worker, the annual earnings increase would of course be larger. If the families of one-third of the affected workers (0.33 percent of all families) are initially poor and are lifted above poverty, then the reduction of poverty would approximately equal the magnitudes implied by the poverty estimates noted in the previous paragraph; although one-third may seem high, earnings gains of $800 or $900 or more are not out of the question. Thus, even coupled with some employment reductions, if a fair amount of the gains from living wages go to low-income families (and even more so if the losses fall more heavily on other families), it is possible that living wages on net lift a detectable number of families above the poverty line.

The results obtained using the total family income information from the ADFs stand in contrast to the results for minimum wages. In Table 7.2, the signs of the estimates are consistent with minimum wages initially reducing poverty. But although there is some evidence that minimum wages appear to reduce the probability that families have below poverty-level earnings (although not statistically significant), the longer-term (i.e., after one year) effects on poverty, based on family income, are small and insignificant.

Finally, the previous two chapters indicated that living wage laws covering employers receiving business assistance drove the effects on wages and employment. Similar results should be expected regarding the effects of living wage laws on poverty. Table 7.3 therefore repeats the income-based poverty analysis from Table 7.2, distinguishing between the effects of contractor-only and business assistance living wage laws.

Table 7.3

Contemporaneous and Lagged Effects of Living Wages on the Probability That Families Have Income Below the Poverty Line, Contractor vs. Business Assistance Living Wage Laws

	Effects on the Probability That Families Have Total Income Below the Poverty Line	
Specification 1:		
Living wage (December)	−0.03	
	(1.46)	
Contractor		6.83**
		(2.67)
Business assistance		−1.02
		(1.68)
Specification 2:		
Living wage, 6-month lag (June)	−1.32	
	(1.67)	
Contractor		1.94
		(3.04)
Business assistance		−3.11*
		(1.89)
Specification 3:		
Living wage, 12-month lag (January)	−3.34*	
	(1.73)	
Contractor		2.58
		(3.04)
Business assistance		−5.38**
		(1.81)
Dataset	ADF	ADF
Sample restrictions	>=25 per cell	>=25 per cell
Years that sample covers	95–99	95–99

NOTES: See the notes to Table 7.2. The sample size is 103,601.

**Significantly different from zero at the 5 percent level.

The estimates in the second column reveal, indeed, that the poverty-reducing effect of living wage laws stems solely from business assistance laws. In particular, for the 12-month lag, the effect (−5.38) is larger than the corresponding estimate in Table 7.2 and strongly statistically significant, whereas the estimated effect of contractor-only laws is small and insignificant. In addition to reflecting what was expected, given the earlier results, this consistency across the various results strengthens the entire set of findings, because the results for poverty come from a different data source and a different measure of the outcome.

Overall, then, the analysis provides some evidence that living wages may be modestly successful at reducing urban poverty in the cities that have adopted such legislation. Viewed through a slightly different prism, the results provide no evidence and indeed sometimes reject the view that living wages increase urban poverty. Thus, although theory makes no predictions regarding the effects of living wages on poverty, the evidence suggests that it is more likely that living wages reduce urban poverty than the opposite.

Results for California

Finally, as in the previous chapters, results are reported for California residents only, in Table 7.4. In this case, in looking at earnings, the estimates reveal stronger effects in reducing urban poverty than are found in the data for the United States as a whole, while the point estimates for income are similar to those for the United States as a whole. Although the earnings estimates are perhaps implausibly large, coupled with the results for the country as a whole, the evidence suggests that living wage laws in California cities have helped urban, low-income families.

Conclusions

Living wage ordinances mandate wage floors that are typically much higher than the wage floors set by state and federal minimum wage legislation. These are frequently tied to the federal government's definition of poverty. Although economic theory offers some guidance as to the expected tradeoffs between employment and higher mandated wage floors, it makes no predictions regarding the effects of living wage laws on poverty. The estimates in earlier chapters indicate that living wage laws—in particular the broader variety that are not restricted to contractors but also cover employers receiving business assistance—raise wages of low-skilled workers but at the cost of some disemployment effects. The estimates in this chapter suggest that the net result is that these living wage ordinances lead to moderate reductions in the likelihood that urban families live in poverty.

Table 7.4

Contemporaneous and Lagged Effects on the Probability That Family Earnings or Income Falls Below the Poverty Line, California Residents Only

	Effects on the Probability That Families Have Total Earnings Below the Poverty Line		Effects on the Probability That Families Have Total Income Below the Poverty Line	
Specification 1:				
Living wage (December)	−8.40**	−7.91**	1.73	−0.34
	(3.38)	(3.97)	(4.19)	(3.46)
Specification 2:				
Living wage, 6-month lag (June)	−11.26**	−11.22**	−1.18	−2.51
	(2.50)	(2.82)	(3.57)	(3.00)
Specification 3:				
Living wage, 12-month lag (January)	−10.83**	−10.17**	−3.04	−3.77
	(2.91)	(3.22)	(3.42)	(3.14)
Dataset	ADF	ADF	ADF	ADF
Sample restrictions	≥ 25 per cell	≥ 25 per cell	≥ 25 per cell	≥ 25 per cell
Years that sample covers	96–99	95–99	96–99	95–99
Number of observations	14,754	18,368	12,050	15,116
Mean percentage below poverty	31.58	31.54	21.90	21.94

NOTES: See the notes to Table 7.2. A total of 22 metropolitan areas are included in the analysis, with the addition of Salinas to the cities listed in the notes to Tables 5.9 and 6.5.

**Significantly different from zero at the 5 percent level.

8. The Effects of Living Wages on Unionized Municipal Workers

The previous chapter focused on assessing the antipoverty effects of living wage laws, noting that fighting poverty is the usual rationale for these laws. However, rather than mandate higher wages for all workers—as a minimum wage does, except for minor coverage exclusions—a curious feature of living wage laws is their frequently narrow coverage. In particular, although some laws cover employers receiving business assistance from the city and even fewer cover city employees, the most common feature is coverage of employers who are contractors or subcontractors with the city. For living wage laws covering contractors or subcontractors, estimates of the percentage of workers affected are quite low. This raises the question of why—given the stated antipoverty objective—living wage laws are focused on raising the wage floors for so few workers, as opposed to creating more general wage floors at the local level.[1]

One possibility is that living wage laws serve other interests, offering higher-paid municipal workers protection *from* low-wage workers, rather than offering protection *for* low-wage workers. In particular, by raising the wages that city contractors must pay, living wage laws may reduce the incentives for cities to contract out work that would otherwise be done by municipal employees. In this sense, living wage laws may parallel the Davis-Bacon Act and other state-level prevailing wage laws affecting

---

[1]Local minimum wage proposals are rare. One is currently under consideration in New Orleans, and proposals were defeated in Houston in 1997 and Denver in 1996. As mentioned in Chapter 1, Santa Monica recently passed a living wage law that combines features of living wages and minimum wages.

public construction projects.[2] It is natural to consider such restrictions as potentially enhancing union bargaining power, and hence in particular protecting or increasing wage premiums or "rents" for municipal union workers, as well as increasing the ability of these workers to prevent contracting out of their jobs. Economists refer to such behavior as "rent-seeking," and hence this chapter refers to the "rent-seeking hypothesis" regarding union support for living wages. Indeed, some evidence reported below suggests that unions representing municipal workers are particularly active in advocating living wage laws, and resolutions from the 1999 AFL-CIO convention note that lifting the wage floor via living wages and other mechanisms "enhances bargaining power and security for all workers."[3]

This last quote succinctly captures the political economy puzzle posed by living wage laws. If the goal is to increase security for all workers—consistent with a broad antipoverty agenda—then why are resources being focused on living wage laws that generally have narrow coverage rather than on broad measures? Or does the emphasis on enhancing bargaining power suggest that a principal effect of living wage laws is to benefit unionized municipal employees who might otherwise face competition from low-wage labor employed by city contractors and subcontractors? This chapter explores the differential effects of living wage laws on different groups of workers, with a particular focus on establishing empirically whether unionized municipal workers gain from living wage laws. Of course, establishing such evidence does not necessarily imply that unionized municipal workers seek to establish living wage laws for their own benefit. Unions may work on behalf of living wage laws for other possible reasons, discussed below, although these hypotheses do not necessarily predict gains for unionized municipal workers. Empirical analysis can be informative about the observed consequences of a particular behavior or policy change but at best can only establish the consistency of the evidence with particular motives.

---

[2]See Kessler and Katz (1999) for an analysis of prevailing wage laws. The less well-known 1965 Service Contract Act also regulates wages paid by contractors providing services to the federal government.

[3]See www.aflcio.org/convention99/res1_l.htm.

Relationship to Earlier Findings

The evidence described in previous chapters suggests that living wage laws boost the wages of low-wage workers, although mainly in the cities in which living wage laws apply to employers receiving business assistance, rather than in the cities with narrower laws restricted to covering contractors, whereas negative employment effects appear to arise in response to the wage increases stemming from the broader living wage laws. In addition, business assistance living wage laws appear to reduce urban poverty.

There are two points to keep in mind in interpreting this earlier evidence coupled with the inquiries taken up in this chapter. First, there is not necessarily any contradiction between finding some beneficial effects for low-wage workers and low-income families, on the one hand, and gains for unionized city employees, on the other. Living wage laws could also benefit low-wage workers or low-income families if the employment and hours responses to wage increases are sufficiently moderate, and the distribution of gains and losses across families tilts the benefits toward poor families.[4] Rather, the rent-seeking perspective is meant to help clarify the political economy of living wage laws, by asking whether there are other motivations for the passage of these laws.

The second point to keep in mind in synthesizing this chapter with the earlier results is that it is the possibility or "threat" of higher wage floors for contractors that is likely to generate benefits for unionized city workers. Thus, contractor living wage laws are the focus of this chapter. Because contractor-only living wage laws do not appear to be associated with benefits for low-wage workers or low-income families, evidence that these types of living wage laws benefit unionized city workers would tend to cast living wage laws limited to restrictions on wages paid by city contractors in a negative light. Furthermore, the fact that contractor-only laws do not result in detectable wage increases for low-wage workers does not imply that unionized municipal workers cannot gain from

---

[4]By way of analogy, unions typically oppose workfare arrangements (work programs for welfare recipients), perhaps because these schemes may increase competition for union labor from low-wage labor. However, some low-wage workers who would suffer from increased competition from workfare participants may also gain from union resistance to workfare.

them. Indeed, the gains to the latter workers would come about because contracting out is deterred, so higher wages for nonunion contractor employees need not be realized for the rent-seeking hypothesis to predict gains for unionized municipal workers.

Implicit in this argument is that the focus of many living wage laws on contractors is consistent with the rent-seeking hypothesis, because it is this particular feature of these laws that is likely to help unionized municipal employees. An alternative view is that contractor-only laws are the easiest to pass because they are more limited, and hence serve as the initial goal of living wage campaigns to be followed later by broader laws. Although this cannot be ruled out, there appear to be no cases of cities that first passed contractor-only living wage laws and subsequently broadened their coverage. Another related possibility is that narrow contractor-only laws result from compromises in which advocates seek broader laws, but narrower ones result because of opposition from employer groups or others. It would be interesting, although difficult, to try to explore the relationship between the role of unions in particular living wage campaigns and whether these campaigns focused more on contractor-only laws, and more generally to try to determine the factors that lead to the passage of different types of living wage laws.

Union Support for Living Wages

The central evidence considered in this chapter is the economic gains that accrue to unionized municipal workers from the implementation of living wage laws. However, if living wage laws partly reflect rent-seeking on the part of municipal unions, we would expect organizations representing unionized municipal workers to be involved in political efforts to pass living wage laws. This section describes some evidence of such activity.

As one method of assessing the involvement of unions with living wage campaigns, a simple set of Internet searches was conducted, looking for joint mention of living wage campaigns and labor unions. This evidence is summarized in Table 8.1. The first column reports the number of hits for "living wage" and the name of each of the 19 cities

Table 8.1

Evidence on Union Involvement in Living Wage Campaigns Based on Internet Search Hits

	Total Hits by City (Name of City + "Living Wage")	Percentage of Total Hits					
		AFL-CIO	AFSCME	SEIU	IBEW	UFCW	HERE
Baltimore	2,560	15.9	6.2	5.2	1.3	1.6	1.8
Boston	5,290	16.0	4.3	5.1	1.4	1.5	1.7
Buffalo	1,300	13.2	5.8	5.0	1.5	2.2	2.2
Chicago	6,140	16.9	4.5	6.3	1.4	1.7	1.7
Dayton	715	15.5	6.4	7.1	1.7	1.3	0.8
Denver	1,760	12.3	4.6	5.5	1.0	1.4	1.1
Detroit	2,980	16.2	5.6	6.8	2.0	2.2	1.9
Durham	676	12.3	5.8	5.3	0.7	2.2	0.9
Hartford	835	16.9	7.1	10.1	1.2	2.0	3.1
Los Angeles	6,650	19.7	4.4	6.9	1.2	1.7	2.8
Milwaukee	1,680	20.5	9.0	8.5	1.8	2.9	2.5
Minneapolis	2,350	12.3	4.7	3.9	0.9	1.4	1.6
Oakland	2,890	13.1	4.2	5.9	1.1	1.8	1.8
Omaha	316	11.7	4.1	4.1	1.3	3.5	1.6
Portland	2,680	10.5	4.3	4.4	1.1	1.5	0.8
San Antonio	1,370	11.9	3.0	3.1	0.8	1.2	1.0
San Francisco	5,960	15.8	4.1	6.1	1.0	1.3	1.7
San Jose	1,600	19.0	6.3	10.1	1.7	2.8	2.1
St. Louis	1,560	16.2	5.3	5.3	1.9	2.2	1.5

NOTES: The Google search engine was used to compile these figures on April 3, 2001. The percentage figures were based on adding the specific union to the search specification. Union abbreviations are as follows: AFL-CIO—American Federation of Labor and Congress of Industrial Organizations; AFSCME—American Federation of State, County, and Municipal Employees; IBEW—International Brotherhood of Electrical Workers; SEIU—Service Employees International Union; UFCW—United Food and Commercial Workers Union; and HERE—Hotel Employees and Restaurant Employees. The acronym for the union was used in all cases except for HERE.

included in the analysis in this chapter.[5] Subsequently, names of various labor organizations were added to the list, beginning with the AFL-CIO, and then, based on preliminary searches of the first set of hits in the first

---

[5]As explained below, the empirical analysis is restricted to city-quarter cells (for cities identified in the CPS) for which there are at least 100 observations in the ORG files. The 19 cities in Table 8-1 are those that have living wage laws and meet this criterion.

column, specific unions that were mentioned often. As shown, a relatively high fraction of hits involving living wages also mentioned the AFL-CIO or a specific labor union. In the absence of information on city contracts—which is difficult to come by—it is not entirely clear which unions might have the most vested interest in living wage laws. However, aside from the AFL-CIO umbrella organization, the largest shares of hits are associated with the two unions that play a prominent role in organizing local government workers: AFSCME and SEIU.[6]

In and of itself, of course, the evidence in Table 8.1 says nothing about support for living wages on the part of unions. However, a casual perusal of the materials uncovered in the search documented in Table 8.1 indicates strong support. A sampling of quotes from these documents is provided in Table 8.2. They clearly document the active advocacy of labor unions in support of living wage campaigns. Although this is not a random sample of quotes, statements paralleling those in Table 8.2 were plentiful, and in a broader and random sample of the Internet sites documented in Table 8.1, no statements by unions in opposition to living wage laws were uncovered.

The evidence presented in Tables 8.1 and 8.2 does not prove that unions back living wage laws as part of a rent-seeking strategy. Unions may have other incentives, such as preferences for less inequality in the wage structure or reductions in poverty. Alternatively, union support for living wage campaigns may provide publicity and contacts, as well as symbolic victories, that prove useful in future organizing drives or in transforming the public image of unions from one of narrow self-interest to one with broader social goals (Nissen, 2000). Nonetheless, although it is probably not possible to discern the exact motives underlying union support for living wages, the evidence of this support at least suggests

---

[6]Of course, the numbers would change from day to day. But comparing these numbers to those obtained five months earlier revealed little qualitative change in the pattern. In addition, different search engines yield different results. To see whether the qualitative conclusions were sensitive, Yahoo and Excite were also used to do the searches for Baltimore. Both had considerably fewer hits (1,120 and 980, respectively). But the percentages accounted for by the various unions revealed similar patterns, with AFSCME and SEIU accounting for at least three times as many hits as the other individual unions.

Table 8.2

Sampling of Quotes Documenting Union Involvement in Living Wage Campaigns

In 1994, after more than a year of coalition building, lobbying and negotiating, AFSCME and the community grassroots organization BUILD (Baltimoreans United in Leadership Development) convinced the city council to pass an ordinance requiring companies that have contracts with the city to pay workers $6.10 an hour (rising to $7.70 this year).

["Transforming Low Pay into a *Living Wage,*" AFL-CIO website, www.aflcio.org/articles/am_at_work/corp_transforming.htm]

A campaign has started in Greensboro to pass a living wage ordinance. The Triad-Central Labor Body is leading the effort. The Triad CLB is a coalition of all area unions affiliated with the AFL-CIO. The CLB is in the early stages of pulling together information and reaching out to local community activists and organizations.

["Living Wage Rage Comes to Greensboro," Pete Castelli, United Needleworkers, Industrial, and Textile Employees, www.ibiblio.org/prism/may98/living.html]

David Newby, State AFL-CIO President, explained why the labor movement was leading the charge for a living wage even though most union members are earning more than the campaign's goal of 110 percent of the poverty level. "The fundamental purpose and goal of unions is to raise the standard of living and the quality of life for all working people. Our basic value is a fair day's wage for a fair day's work," said Newby.

["Living Wage Campaigns: National Trend, Local Focus," *Living Wage Reporter,* Oct./Nov. 1997, www.solidarity.com/LivingWage/Oct.%2097.htm#Living Wage Campaigns: National Trend, Local Focus]

Things are looking up in New Orleans, where an August court date has finally been set to determine the constitutionality of a Louisiana law prohibiting enactment of local living wage ordinances. The law was passed after ACORN and SEIU Local 100 collected enough signatures to put the living wage on the ballot in New Orleans back in 1996.

["Living Wage Campaigns Rage on in ACORN Cities and States," *ACORN Report,* July 1999, www.acorn.org/acorn-reports/acornrep.livingwage.content.html]

The Los Angeles living wage initiative has been led by the Los Angeles Alliance for a New Economy (LAANE). LAANE is a non-profit organization created by the Hotel Employees and Restaurant Employees Union (HERE) Local 11 in 1993 with the goal of creating a more favorable climate for organizing low-wage workers in Los Angeles' second largest sector, the tourism industry.

[*Living Wage Campaigns in the Economic Policy Arena: Four Case Studies from California,* Carol Zabin and Isaac Martin, Center for Labor Research and Education, Institute of Industrial Relations, University of California, Berkeley, June 1999, www.phoenixfund.org/livingwage.htm]

that the rent-seeking hypothesis may be plausible. With that in mind, the next section turns to the central analysis of this chapter, exploring the economic consequences of living wage laws for unionized municipal employees.

Dependent Variables and Hypotheses to Be Tested

Two dependent variables are considered. The first is the share of unionized municipal workers in the city's workforce. Because of the relatively small number of unionized municipal workers, this city-level share is constructed by quarter. If living wage laws actually reduce the extent to which cities contract out jobs, by reducing the incentives of cities to do so, then increases in this share in response to living wage laws might be observed. However, this is a relatively "strong" form of the rent-seeking hypothesis. Instead, what living wage laws may do is reduce the ability of cities negotiating with unionized workers to threaten to contract out work (or reduce the credibility of such threats). This would increase the bargaining power of unions and hence result in higher wages. But it may result in little change in actual contracting out behavior, because the threat need not be carried out (at least, not often) to affect bargaining. Thus, the "weaker" form of the rent-seeking hypothesis is that living wage laws boost the wages of unionized municipal workers.[7]

To parallel the workforce share analysis, the empirical analysis of wages is also done using city-level data.[8] Attention is focused on the

---

[7]Indeed, in a standard model in which employment is determined from the demand curve based on the negotiated wage, such wage gains could generate some employment reductions (and still be preferred by unions if the median union voter values the higher wages), offsetting potential positive effects on the union-municipal workforce share from deterring contracting out. But with public sector unions, wage and employment determination could be quite different, as unionized municipal workers also vote for public officials.

[8]This raises the question of whether the results from the earlier chapters are robust to aggregating the data as is done in this chapter. To explore this, the data aggregated to a city-quarter basis were used to attempt to replicate the basic results on the effects of living wages on low-wage workers, and yielded similar findings. Specifically, with a lag of about one year, living wages boost the average wages of those below the 10th centile of the wage distribution (of the appropriate city-quarter cell), with an elasticity of approximately 0.04. When attention is restricted to living wage laws with broader

wages of unionized municipal workers who earn lower wages, because they are more likely to face competition from lower-wage nonunion labor hired by city contractors and, conversely, to benefit from raising the wage floor for this labor. In particular, the dependent variable used is the average wage of below-median wage (relative to their city-quarter) unionized municipal workers.

The hypothesis that living wages protect unionized municipal workers from lower-wage workers stems from the application of most living wage laws to city contractors and subcontractors. Consequently, most of the empirical analysis focuses on the subset of cities with contractor living wage laws.

The two hypotheses will be tested using a straightforward difference-in-differences framework, as in the previous three chapters. In this framework, the effect of living wages—the treatment—is identified from how changes over time in cities implementing (or raising) living wages differ from changes over the same time span in cities without (or not raising) living wages. Using data for city-quarter cells indexed by city c in quarter q and year y, and denoting city, year, and quarter dummy variables by C, Y, and Q, the baseline regression estimated for each dependent variable (generically denoted y) is of the form

$$
\begin{aligned}
y_{cqy} = {} & \alpha + \beta \ln (w_{cqy}^{min}) + \gamma \max [\ln (w_{cqy}^{liv}), \ln (w_{cqy}^{min})] \\
& + C_c \delta_C + Y_y \theta_Y + Q_q \lambda_Q + \varepsilon_{cqy}.
\end{aligned}
\tag{8.1}
$$

Descriptive Statistics on Workers

Central to the analysis in this chapter is the classification of workers by union status and municipal employment. Municipal workers are identified from the "class of worker" variable in the CPS, which refers to the primary job. Having restricted the sample to those living in metropolitan areas, those working for "local government" are considered municipal employees, although some may work for other units of government below the state level. Union status is based on whether the

---

coverage extending to employers receiving business assistance, the elasticity increases to nearly 0.08.

individual reports being a "member of a labor union or an employee association similar to a union."

Table 8.3 provides some descriptive information on workers classified by municipal employment and union status, detailing their occupational distribution. In addition, because living wage laws are likely to affect lower-wage workers, these descriptive statistics are presented for those workers earning below the median wage in the corresponding city-quarter cell. The first row of numbers in the table describes the workforce share of workers classified by union status and municipal employment. Looking first at all workers, the overall unionization rate in these data is 0.145, with 29 percent of union workers employed by municipalities. When attention is restricted to those earning below the median wage, the unionization rate drops, reflecting the fact that union workers generally earn higher wages. The share of unionized municipal workers among this subset is particularly small, representing 1.9 percent of these lower-wage workers. This low share highlights the inherent difficulty of using CPS data to study a group of workers as narrow as unionized workers employed by municipalities, in particular highlighting the relatively small number of workers from whom the effects of living wage laws can be identified.[9]

The remaining rows of the table provide information on the occupational breakdown of workers based on union status and municipal employment. Each column reports the distribution of workers in that column. Looking first at all workers, the heaviest concentration of unionized municipal workers is among teachers, accounting for 41.3 percent of these workers. There are also high concentrations among executives, professionals excluding teachers, and police, as well as clerical workers, those in other services, and craft workers. Among workers earning below the median wage, unionized municipal workers are much more concentrated among clerical workers and workers in other services;

---

[9]Specifically, consider the analysis of wage effects on unionized municipal workers in affected occupations, earning below median wages. For this analysis, there are 1,075 observations on individual workers in the control sample of cities never passing living wage laws. In the treatment sample in which living wages are passed, there are 306 observations before the implementation of the living wage, and 353 afterward.

Table 8.3

Distribution of Workers by Unionization, Municipal Employment, and Major Occupation

	All Workers				Workers Below Median Wage			
	U,M	U,NM	NU,M	NU,NM	U,M	U,NM	NU,M	NU,NM
Workforce share:	0.042	0.103	0.043	0.813	0.019	0.064	0.040	0.877
Occupations:								
Executive, administrative	0.055	0.052	0.145	0.161	0.028	0.026	0.057	0.073
Professional, excluding teachers	0.093	0.078	0.121	0.121	0.053	0.026	0.059	0.041
Teachers	0.413	0.046	0.195	0.025	0.230	0.023	0.128	0.023
Technical	0.013	0.031	0.023	0.040	0.012	0.022	0.021	0.025
Sales	0.003	0.051	0.010	0.134	0.007	0.101	0.017	0.150
Clerical	0.127	0.148	0.217	0.157	0.313	0.165	0.324	0.194
Private household	0.000	0.001	0.000	0.007	0.000	0.002	0.000	0.012
Protective services, excluding police and fire	0.007	0.006	0.016	0.008	0.018	0.013	0.027	0.011
Police	0.095	0.012	0.044	0.001	0.035	0.003	0.022	0.001
Fire	0.036	0.001	0.009	0.000	0.023	0.001	0.007	0.000
Other services	0.062	0.090	0.121	0.116	0.179	0.200	0.228	0.194
Craft	0.041	0.208	0.037	0.090	0.024	0.093	0.026	0.078
Machine operator	0.003	0.117	0.004	0.055	0.004	0.139	0.005	0.075
Transportation	0.036	0.080	0.033	0.031	0.051	0.061	0.041	0.039
Handler	0.011	0.075	0.011	0.039	0.016	0.120	0.018	0.062
Farming, fishery	0.006	0.005	0.013	0.014	0.009	0.009	0.020	0.022

NOTES: U,M—unionized, municipal; U,NM—unionized, nonmunicipal; NU,M—nonunionized, municipal; NU,NM—nonunionized, nonmunicipal. Occupational distribution shows the share in each category of workers (e.g., unionized, municipal) in each listed occupation. Sample-weighted estimated proportions are reported. Medians are estimated by city-quarter cell using sample weights. The sample is restricted to individuals residing in metropolitan areas. The sample size is 375,483. The sample size for observations below the (weighted) median is 183,315.

together, these two occupations constitute 49.2 percent of unionized municipal workers earning below-median wages. Aside from the likelihood that living wage laws are likely to affect lower-wage workers, this provides another motivation for restricting attention to those earning below median wages. In particular, for some occupations—most obviously teachers, police, and fire—because of the inability of municipalities to contract out, unionized municipal workers seem unlikely to need living wage laws to be protected from competition from lower-wage, typically nonunion labor. Thus, most of the analysis is restricted to occupations other than these three.

Table 8.4 reports descriptive information on wages by union status, municipal employment, and occupation. There are no real surprises here in terms of wage differentials by occupation, union status, or municipal employment. What is informative, though, is a comparison of some of these wages with legislated living wages (reported in Tables 1.1 and 1.3). In particular, once attention is restricted to those earning below-median wages, average wages for most occupations appear to be in the range where living wages might pose a binding constraint for a reasonable fraction of nonunionized, nonmunicipal workers. At the same time, the wage floors imposed by living wages are close enough to the wages of unionized municipal workers that it might be possible to detect benefits to them from living wages, if these benefits exist. In contrast, the average wages of unionized municipal workers overall are sufficiently high that it seems less plausible that living wage laws would have a detectable effect on the higher-wage members of this set of workers.

Descriptive Statistics on Cities

Having provided some descriptive information on unionized municipal workers, Table 8.5 reports descriptive statistics for the city-level data used in the empirical analysis. The sample is restricted to city-quarter cells in which there are at least 100 observations overall, in an attempt to increase the accuracy of the estimates; even so, these cells frequently contain very few unionized municipal workers.

The first panel provides some general information on wages for cities with any living wage laws before and after the initial implementation of

Table 8.4

Average Wages of Workers by Unionization, Municipal Employment, and Major Occupation

Occupations	All Workers				Workers Below Median Wage			
	U,M	U,NM	NU,M	NU,NM	U,M	U,NM	NU,M	NU,NM
Executive, administrative	20.09	18.72	18.39	18.82	10.66	10.08	8.53	8.95
Professional, excluding teachers	20.26	20.81	17.42	20.19	10.46	9.91	8.45	8.71
Teachers	19.87	19.51	14.18	13.82	10.28	9.61	8.05	7.63
Technical	16.19	21.19	12.48	15.06	10.80	10.17	8.34	8.92
Sales	13.01	10.82	8.25	12.03	8.84	7.82	6.80	6.85
Clerical	11.85	13.58	9.47	10.30	9.45	9.61	7.68	8.10
Private household	...	6.49	...	6.67	...	6.49	...	5.88
Protective services, excluding police and fire	12.13	10.92	7.92	8.37	9.20	8.11	6.69	6.94
Police	19.16	17.64	14.17	16.64	11.18	10.42	8.61	9.82
Fire	16.43	15.27	12.80	12.98	9.38	9.03	7.63	7.49
Other services	10.62	10.67	7.33	6.70	8.86	8.01	6.59	6.00
Craft	16.72	17.58	13.24	12.19	10.69	9.78	8.23	8.27
Machine operator	14.62	13.16	10.77	8.49	10.20	8.76	6.97	7.27
Transportation	13.56	15.15	9.89	9.64	10.29	9.67	7.97	7.71
Handler	13.83	11.85	8.22	7.54	10.07	7.92	7.03	6.75
Farming, fishery	13.04	11.12	8.65	7.21	9.76	8.46	6.76	6.44

NOTES: See the notes to Table 8.3. Wage measures (except living wages and minimum wages) are deflated by the average hourly earnings series and are expressed in 1996:Q1 dollars.

Table 8.5

Descriptive Statistics

	Cities with Any Living Wage Law		Contractor Living Wage Laws		No Living Wage Law
	Before	After	Before	After	Law
General wage measures	N=175	N=176	N=156	N=145	N=822
Average living wage	4.81	7.66	4.83	7.58	5.02
	(0.40)	(0.72)	(0.40)	(0.70)	(0.37)
Average minimum wage	4.81	5.35	4.83	5.38	5.02
	(0.40)	(0.40)	(0.46)	(0.41)	(0.37)
Average wage	11.88	11.97	11.94	11.93	11.32
	(1.34)	(1.43)	(1.29)	(1.39)	(1.45)
Average wage, workers below 10th centile	5.70	5.76	5.71	5.71	5.53
	(0.57)	(0.66)	(0.57)	(0.64)	(0.52)
Unionized municipal workers					
Proportion of workforce unionized, municipal	0.044	0.049	0.043	0.050	0.042
	(0.020)	(0.017)	(0.021)	(0.017)	(0.031)
Excluding teachers, police, fire	0.022	0.026	0.022	0.026	0.020
	(0.016)	(0.013)	(0.016)	(0.018)	(0.020)
Workers with wage below median	0.015	0.018	0.015	0.017	0.014
	(0.015)	(0.015)	(0.014)	(0.015)	(0.017)
Average wage of unionized municipal workers—excluding teachers, police, and fire—with wage below median	9.31	9.26	9.26	9.15	9.16
	(1.68)	(1.38)	(1.68)	(1.35)	(1.77)
	N=117	N=132	N=107	N=114	N=434
Average number of individuals per cell	243.9	275.7	254.1	292.4	194.7

NOTES: Data used are means computed over city-quarter cells. Standard deviations are reported in parentheses. Sample includes all city-quarter cells with at least 100 observations (for all workers). Living wage variable is the higher of living wage or minimum wage, averaged over the quarter. Wage measures (except living wages and minimum wages) are deflated by the average hourly earnings series and are expressed in 1996:Q1 dollars. Centiles of wage distribution are calculated for each city-quarter cell. Estimates are weighted, with workforce share variables weighted by overall city-quarter cell size and wage variables weighted by the number of corresponding observations in the cell. "After" includes quarters in which the living wage increased and all quarters afterward. Sample sizes (number of city-quarter cells) in the top row apply to all rows except for wage figures for unionized workers, where sample sizes can be smaller if there are no workers satisfying the indicated criteria; separate sample sizes are reported for these cells.

the living wage, for the same breakdown focusing only on living wage laws covering contractors, and for cities with no living wage laws in the sample period. The wage figures are deflated by the average hourly earnings series, with the first quarter of 1996 used as the base. These figures suggest that living wages (either in total or only covering contractors) were implemented in cities with wages that were higher by about 5 percent and with wages of workers below the 10th centile that were higher by about 3 percent.

The second panel first provides information on the workforce share of unionized municipal workers. The figures indicate that whether looking at the workforce overall, at "affected" occupations (excluding teachers, police, and fire), or at the subset of workers in these occupations with below median wages, living wages were implemented in cities with only slightly higher representation of unionized municipal workers. For example, in the latter case, this workforce share was 0.015 in cities that later passed a living wage law covering contractors, as compared to 0.014 in cities that never passed a living wage law. This suggests that there was little difference between the treatment and control groups before the implementation of living wages, although this issue is explored further in the regression analysis that follows. In addition, for the treatment group, each of the workforce share measures is slightly higher in the post-living wage period. Of course, this may not hold in the regression analysis, which accounts for common changes over time and city-specific differences in these workforce shares; in contrast, these changes and differences can affect the estimates in Table 8.5 because different cities are in the "Before" and "After" columns for different numbers of quarters.

The last row of the second panel reports average wages for the group of workers that will be the focus of the analysis, those earning below-median wages, excluding teachers, police, and fire. These figures indicate that living wages were implemented in cities in which these workers earned only slightly higher wages (about 1 percent), again suggesting similarity of the treatment and control groups. These figures fail to reveal any wage increase for these workers following the implementation of a living wage, although, as noted above, this result can easily change in the regression analysis. On the other hand, note that the standard deviation is substantially lower following the implementation of a living wage, suggesting some effect on wages.

Effects of Living Wage Laws on the Workforce Share of Unionized Municipal Workers

Having laid this groundwork, the next two sections report results on explicit tests of the rent-seeking explanation of living wages. The first analysis focuses on the strong test, asking whether living wage laws boost the workforce share of unionized municipal workers; the second focuses on the weak test, estimating the effects of these laws on the wages of unionized municipal workers.

The results of this first analysis are reported in Table 8.6. They can be summarized quite succinctly; there is no statistical evidence that living wage laws affect the share of the workforce consisting of unionized municipal workers. The first three columns examine the effect of living wage laws on this workforce share among all these workers. The remaining columns exclude teachers, police, and fire, and the final column focuses on those earning below-median wages. In each column, three separate specifications are estimated, using the contemporaneous living wage variable (and minimum wage variable), followed by a specification with six-month (two-quarter) lags, and a specification with 12-month (four-quarter) lags. These alternative lags allow the effects to take place some time after a living wage is implemented or increased. For example, in the chapters above, the effects of living wages on wages, employment, and also family income took about one year to appear. In all three columns, for each specification, the estimated effect is statistically insignificant. The same is true in the next two columns where the specification of the wage floor is altered, first by dropping the minimum wage variable so that a single wage floor is included in the model, and then by instead substituting the difference (in logs) between the living wage and the minimum wage. Finally, given the small number of unionized municipal workers in the dataset, there may be an excessive number of observations with a measured workforce share of unionized municipal workers equal to zero. To assess whether the estimates are sensitive to this, the specifications are reestimated using only those city-

Table 8.6

Effects of Contractor Living Wage Laws on Workforce Share of Unionized Municipal Workers

	All Workers	Excluding Teachers, Police, Fire	Excluding Teachers, Police, Fire, Below Median Wage	Excluding Teachers, Police, Fire, Below Median Wage	Excluding Teachers, Police, Fire, Below Median Wage, Cities with Positive Share in All Months
Contemporaneous specification:					
Living wage	0.005	0.005	0.003	0.005	0.003
	(0.005)	(0.004)	(0.004)	(0.004)	(0.005)
Minimum wage	0.029	0.004	0.011	...	0.005
	(0.014)	(0.011)	(0.012)		(0.014)
Living wage – minimum wage	...	...	...	0.004	...
				(0.004)	
6-month lag specification:					
Living wage	0.006	0.001	0.004	0.005	0.003
	(0.006)	(0.004)	(0.005)	(0.004)	(0.005)
Minimum wage	0.002	-0.002	0.006	...	-0.005
	(0.016)	(0.011)	(0.012)		(0.014)
Living wage – minimum wage	...	...	...	0.005	...
				(0.005)	
12-month lag specification:					
Living wage	0.003	-0.003	-0.001	0.003	-0.002
	(0.006)	(0.004)	(0.006)	(0.005)	(0.006)
Minimum wage	0.013	0.011	0.018	...	0.017
	(0.016)	(0.012)	(0.013)		(0.015)
Living wage – minimum wage	...	...	...	0.000	...
				(0.006)	
Sample size	1,123	1,123	1,123	1,123	624

NOTES: See the notes to Table 8.5. In addition to reported variables, specifications include dummy variables for city, year, and quarter. Estimates are weighted by overall city-quarter cell size. Results are reported using the wage floor applicable when health insurance is provided. The estimates were very similar using the higher wage floor. When the contemporaneous, 6-month, and 12-month lags were included simultaneously, tests of joint significance of the living wage or minimum wage effects, and of the sums of the living wage or minimum wage effects, were insignificant.

119

quarter cells with nonzero observations for this workforce share, which cuts the sample size nearly in half. Regardless, there is still no evidence of an effect of living wages on the workforce share of unionized municipal workers.[10]

One reason to avoid drawing strong conclusions from these results may be that it would not be possible to detect significant effects of plausible magnitudes in these data. For example, as Table 8.5 shows, the mean of the workforce share for the sample used in the third column, which provides perhaps the best experiment by focusing on affected workers in the lower wage ranges, is 0.014 (in the cities with no living wage). The standard error on the regression coefficient in Table 8.6 is 0.006 for the 12-month lag specification. Thus, if a living wage were imposed that was 50 percent higher than the minimum wage, even if this ultimately raised the workforce share of unionized municipal workers by, for example, 0.004 (a 29 percent increase, which seems quite large), the estimated effect would not be statistically significant. Conversely, coefficients of the magnitudes reported, if significant, would represent sizable effects. As an example, in the specification including and then summing the contemporaneous and the two lagged effects (not reported in the table), the standard error of the sum is 0.006, but the estimated coefficient is 0.003, which would imply that a 50 percent increase in the living wage would boost the workforce share of unionized municipal workers by 11 percent, a large increase that would not be statistically significant. Thus, the analysis of the effects of living wage laws on the workforce share of unionized municipal workers should perhaps be regarded more as uninformative than as suggesting that living wage laws do not boost this share.

Effects of Living Wage Laws on the Wages of Unionized Municipal Workers

Finally, the focus shifts to the empirical test of the rent-seeking hypothesis that is more likely to reveal beneficial effects of living wages for unionized municipal workers, if such effects are present, namely,

---

[10]The models were also estimated as Tobits, to account for the truncation at zero, but the results were very similar.

whether living wages boost wages of these workers. The basic results are reported in Table 8.7, as noted before for below median wage unionized municipal workers in occupations excluding teachers, police, and fire.

The first three panels of the table report estimates from separate specifications using alternatively contemporaneous, six-month lags, and 12-month lags of the living wage and minimum wage variables. As in Table 8.6, across the columns specifications are also reported dropping the minimum wage variable and using only the difference between the living wage and the minimum wage. The results in the three columns are very consistent. The contemporaneous effect of the living wage on the wages of unionized municipal workers is large, with an elasticity of about 0.13, and statistically significant. The six-month lag specifications still point to positive effects, although smaller and no longer statistically significant, consistent with some moderation of the wage effect (although this is easily attributable to sampling variation as well). The 12-month lag specifications point to somewhat larger effects, statistically significant at the 10 percent level in two of the three specifications. In contrast, the minimum wage effects, in the first column, are always statistically insignificant and imprecisely estimated.

Given the generally persistent effects of living wages, the last panel includes simultaneously the contemporaneous and two lagged living wage variables (and the corresponding minimum wage variables) and reports their overall statistical significance and, most important, the estimated summed effect and standard error of the sum. All three specifications point to relatively large and statistically significant positive effects of living wages on the wages of unionized municipal workers, with elasticities in the 0.14 to 0.16 range. These estimates imply, for example, that implementation of a living wage that exceeds the minimum wage by 50 percent would raise wages of these workers by approximately 7.5 percent.

The evidence in Table 8.7 would have to be summarized as providing relatively strong support for the hypothesis that living wages offer lower-wage unionized municipal employees some protection from

Table 8.7

Effects of Contractor Living Wage Laws on Average Wages of Below Median Wage Unionized Municipal Workers

Contemporaneous specification:			
Living wage	0.134**	0.131**	...
	(0.062)	(0.057)	
Minimum wage	−0.031	...	...
	(0.170)		
Living wage − minimum wage	...	...	0.135**
			(0.062)
R^2	0.474	0.474	0.473
6-month lag specification:			
Living wage	0.076	0.057	...
	(0.063)	(0.058)	
Minimum wage	−0.131	...	...
	(0.159)		
Living wage − minimum wage	...	...	0.075
			(0.063)
12-month lag specification:			
Living wage	0.112*	0.096	...
	(0.067)	(0.064)	
Minimum wage	−0.102	...	...
	(0.186)		
Living wage − minimum wage	...	...	0.113*
			(0.067)
Including contemporaneous, 6-month, and 12-month lags of living wages and minimum wages:			
Living wage variables			
Joint significance (p-value)	0.049	0.040	0.073
Sum	0.164**	0.142**	0.163**
(Standard error)	(0.077)	(0.072)	(0.077)
Minimum wage variables			
Joint significance (p-value)	0.823	...	...
Sum	−0.140	...	...
(Standard error)	(0.209)		
Sample size	655	655	655

NOTES: See the notes to Tables 8.5 and 8.6. Estimates are weighted by the number of observations in the cell used to construct the wage measure.

*Significantly different from zero at the 10 percent level.

**Significantly different from zero at the 5 percent level.

low-wage labor.[11] To further explore the validity of this result, and its sensitivity and robustness, Tables 8.8 and 8.9 present results from a variety of alternative analyses. In most cases, results are reported from the specifications including the contemporaneous, six-month, and 12-month lags of the living wage variable—first, also with the corresponding minimum wage variable, and then using the difference from the minimum wage variable.

The analyses presented in Table 8.8 explore the possibility that the positive estimated effects of living wages on the wages of unionized municipal workers are spurious. A spurious effect could arise because of coincidental changes in wages for workers in the wage range of unionized municipal workers, or perhaps because cities simultaneously pass living wage laws and increase the wages paid to their own workers. The evidence in Table 8.8 is based on specifications similar to those just reported. However, it focuses on various groups of workers whose wages should *not* be affected by living wage laws under the rent-seeking hypothesis (that is, not treatment groups), but might nonetheless be driven by some of these same sources of a spurious effect. If the effects for unionized municipal employees just discussed are real and not spurious, similar effects should *not* appear for these other groups of workers.

In the first column, attention is restricted to unionized municipal workers earning below-median wages, as before, but now looking exclusively at teachers, police, and fire. Workers in these occupations were excluded above because they seem unlikely to face competition from lower-wage nonunion labor, but they nonetheless constitute 28.8 percent of unionized municipal workers with below median wages. The estimates indicate no effect of living wages on the wages paid to this group; the estimated coefficients are negative, rather than positive, insignificantly different from zero, and imprecise.

---

[11]This evidence remained when the analysis was repeated allowing for different trends in the cities that passed living wage laws in the sample period and those that did not, which had no qualitative effect upon the conclusions. In principle, the positive wage effects could arise from employment losses among the lowest-wage unionized municipal workers, but no adverse employment effects were detected in Table 8.6.

Table 8.8

Estimates of Effects of Contractor Living Wages on Average Wages, "Nontreatment" Groups, Below Median Wage Workers

	Contractor Living Wage Laws				Noncontractor Living Wage Laws
	U,M, Teachers, Police, and Fire Only	U,NM	NU,M	NU,NM	U,M, Excluding Teachers, Police, and Fire
Including contemporaneous, 6-month, and 12-month lags:					
Living wage variables					
Sum	−0.175	−0.037	−0.022	0.005	−0.106
(Standard error)	(0.215)	(0.051)	(0.075)	(0.023)	(0.114)
Minimum wage variables					
Sum	0.113	0.044	−0.002	0.093	0.180
(Standard error)	(0.512)	(0.131)	(0.224)	(0.064)	(0.291)
Including contemporaneous, 6-month, and 12-month lags:					
Living wage – minimum wage variables					
Sum	−0.190	−0.036	−0.024	0.012	−0.106
(Standard error)	(0.211)	(0.051)	(0.074)	(0.023)	(0.117)
Sample size	388	1,023	1,018	1,123	462

NOTE: See the notes to Table 8.7. U,M—unionized, municipal; U,NM—unionized, nonmunicipal; NU,M—nonunionized, municipal; NU,NM—nonunionized, nonmunicipal.

The next three columns turn to the three other groups of workers classified by union status and municipal employment. In this case, teachers, police, and fire are included because they represent much smaller shares of these groups. For none of the three groups is there evidence that living wage laws boost wages. In these regressions, the estimates are relatively precise and insignificantly different from zero. Finally, the last column returns to the unionized municipal workers in the affected occupations that were analyzed above. However, in this case

Table 8.9

Estimates of Effects of Contractor Living Wages on Average Wages, "Nontreatment" Groups, Sensitivity Analysis, in Cities with Contractor Living Wage Laws, Unionized Municipal Workers (Excluding Teachers, Police, and Fire)

	Occupations with Average Wages < $8.25 per Hour (1)	Wages Below Specified Centile						Add 18-Month Lag (8)	Same Sample as (8), 12-Month Lags Only (9)
		30th (2)	40th (3)	60th (4)	70th (5)	80th (6)	90th (7)		
Including contemporaneous, 6-month, and 12-month lags:									
Living wage variables									
Sum	0.176**	0.026	0.091	0.157**	0.138**	0.072	−0.003	0.186*	0.179**
(Standard error)	(0.087)	(0.109)	(0.085)	(0.067)	(0.065)	(0.071)	(0.075)	(0.095)	(0.081)
Minimum wage variables									
Sum	0.004	−0.144	0.013	−0.369*	−0.224	−0.152	−0.054	−0.182	−0.217
(Standard error)	(0.227)	(0.415)	(0.270)	(0.189)	(0.190)	(0.193)	(0.197)	(0.266)	(0.232)
Including contemporaneous, 6-month, and 12-month lags:									
Living wage − minimum wage variables									
Sum	0.185**	0.017	0.098	0.144**	0.132**	0.065	−0.009	0.190**	0.178**
(Standard error)	(0.086)	(0.111)	(0.085)	(0.067)	(0.066)	(0.071)	(0.073)	(0.095)	(0.081)
Sample size	608	339	498	755	823	864	900	584	584

NOTES: See the notes to Tables 8.5 through 8.7. Except in columns (2) through (7), the sample is also restricted to below median wage workers. Based on Table 8.4, column (8), the occupations excluded from column the first column include executive, administrative, professional (excluding teachers), technical, and craft personnel, in addition to teachers, police, and fire.

*Significantly different from zero at the 10 percent level.

**Significantly different from zero at the 5 percent level

attention is restricted to the few living wage laws that do *not* cover city contractors. In these instances, we would not expect to see any effect on the wages of unionized municipal workers under the rent-seeking hypothesis, whereas if cities implement living wages and wage increases simultaneously, a positive wage effect should still appear.[12] This is confirmed in the estimated effect on wages, which is negative and not significantly different from zero (and rather imprecise, given the small number of cities with such living wage laws).

Overall, then, the evidence in Table 8.8, coupled with the evidence in Table 8.7, indicates that positive effects of contractor living wage laws appear for the group of workers for which such effects would be predicted by the rent-seeking hypothesis, and not for other groups of workers for whom no effects should arise. This suggests that the evidence for the rent-seeking hypothesis stems from the actual effects of contractor living wage laws.

Table 8.9 turns instead to some sensitivity analyses of the result for unionized municipal workers, asking whether the positive wage effect for them persists in alternative specifications, with different sample restrictions, etc. Column (1) deals with a subset of affected occupations with the lowest average wages, specifically wages below $8.25 for nonunion, nonmunicipal workers (see Table 8.4). Unless for some reason these particular occupations are not open to competition from city contractors, it would be expected that the positive wage effect of living wage laws would be present for this group of occupations, and most likely larger. This is confirmed by the estimates, which are slightly larger than the comparable estimates in Table 8.7 and which are statistically significant.[13]

---

[12]This is also true for the estimates using nonunionized municipal workers in the third column of the table.

[13]As a general matter, by restricting the analysis to those with below median wages (in their city-quarter cell), or any other cutoff, it is conceivable that some workers whose wages were raised by living wage laws are dropped, which could introduce some slight downward bias in the estimated effects of living wage laws on the wages of unionized municipal workers. However, this would not alter the conclusion; the results would only be stronger in the absence of this bias. Nonetheless, the estimates should be interpreted carefully, as simply measuring the effect on the average wage of workers whose wages are below the specified cutoff, rather than as measuring a population regression function.

Columns (2) through (7) consider alternative maximum cutoffs for unionized municipal workers, substituting centiles ranging from the 30th to the 90th for the median. The results indicate that at the extremes, the positive effect on wages becomes small and insignificant, but that evidence of this effect is present as long as the range extends through the middle part of the wage distribution.

Finally, the last two columns add another lag of the living wage (and minimum wage) to see whether any evidence exists that the positive effect of living wages weakens over time. In fact, the point estimate adding effects through the 18-month lag is the same or a shade larger than the comparable estimate using lags only through 12 months.

Overall, the positive effect of living wage laws on the wages of lower-wage unionized municipal workers persists in many of the sensitivity analyses reported in Table 8.9. Nonetheless, the combined evidence in columns (2) through (8) points to some fragility or perhaps "narrowness" of the inference that living wage laws boost the wages of unionized municipal workers, and it remains an open question why the lowest-wage workers among these unionized municipal employees appear not to benefit from living wage laws. Unfortunately, the dataset is not large enough to support highly disaggregated analyses that might shed further light on this question.

Conclusions

Living wage laws, which were introduced in the mid-1990s and have expanded rapidly, are typically touted as antipoverty measures. Yet they

---

An alternative that avoids this problem is to use the predicted wage distribution rather than the actual wage distribution. The cost of using this distribution is the inclusion in this lower range of more potentially unaffected workers, thus also biasing any positive effects downward. The same specifications were estimated using the predicted wage distribution and the results were very similar.

A second alternative is to analyze lower-wage occupations without a wage cutoff, although given that there are numerous high-wage workers even in the lower-wage occupations, this is more likely to include unaffected workers and hence obscure the living wage effect. Thus, the wage equation was also estimated for the lower-wage occupations considered in column (1) of Table 8.9, without the median wage cutoff. The estimated wage effects were still positive but about half as large and not statistically significant.

frequently restrict coverage to employers with city contracts and in such cases apply to a small fraction of workers. Because the antipoverty goals would appear to call for broader wage floors, a natural question is whether there are alternative motivations for various economic and political actors to seek passage of living wage laws covering city contractors.

This chapter considers the hypothesis that unions representing municipal employees work for the implementation of living wage laws as a rent-seeking activity. In particular, the hypothesis is that by raising the wages that city contractors would have to pay, living wage laws may reduce the incentives for cities to contract out work that would otherwise be done by municipal employees, hence increasing the bargaining power of municipal unions and leading to higher wages (and perhaps also higher unionization rates). The evidence that labor unions, especially those representing municipal workers, are active in the movement to pass living wage laws favors the rent-seeking hypothesis, although this evidence is only suggestive. The main contribution of this chapter is an empirical analysis of the effects of living wage laws on unionized municipal workers.

Although there is no strong evidence that living wage laws boost the workforce share of unionized municipal workers, there is rather strong evidence that the wages of these workers are increased as a result of living wages. In particular, focusing attention on unionized municipal workers in the lower to middle part of the wage distribution in their local labor market, and on occupations most likely to be affected, the evidence indicates elasticities of average wages with respect to living wages in the 0.1 to 0.15 range. This finding generally holds up in a variety of sensitivity analyses. On the other hand, comparisons of estimated effects for unionized municipal workers that should be affected by living wages with estimated effects for alternative groups of workers that should not experience any effect uniformly indicate positive effects only for the former, making more plausible a causal interpretation of the estimated effects of living wage laws on unionized municipal workers.

The evidence that unionized municipal workers gain from living wage laws does not imply that living wages offer no assistance to low-wage workers or low-income families. Indeed, there is evidence (reported in the chapters above) that living wage laws help to achieve these goals, although more so when they are not narrowly restricted to cover only city contractors but instead extend to employers receiving business assistance from the city. Thus, this evidence should not be interpreted as condemning living wage laws as nothing but a ploy for unionized municipal workers to protect themselves against competition from lower-wage labor that cities might access through contracting out. However, it does add to the literature on "political economy" explanations of labor market and other policies (e.g., Brock and Magee, 1978; Goldin, 1994; Fishback and Kantor, 1998). Moreover, it may help in understanding the evolution of living wage laws and, in particular, the narrow coverage restrictions they frequently entail that appear to undermine the anti-poverty effects of living wages while still delivering benefits to unionized municipal workers.

9. Conclusions

The movement to implement living wage laws in cities across the United States has emerged as a prominent area of political and economic struggle in the past few years. Since the first living wage law passed in Baltimore in 1994, nearly 40 cities and a number of other jurisdictions have followed suit. California has been at the forefront of the campaign, with living wage laws currently in effect in 10 cities that impose some of the highest wage floors in the country, and campaigns under way in other cities as well.

Living wage laws are distinguished by three features. First, all living wage ordinances feature a minimum wage floor that is higher—and often much higher—than the traditional minimum wages set by state and federal legislation. Second, living wage laws frequently link the wage floor to a poverty threshold, for example, requiring a wage that would raise a family of four to the poverty level, assuming one full-time worker. Third, coverage by living wage ordinances is far from universal. The feature common to most living wage laws is to specify coverage of companies under contract with the city. Other living wage laws also impose the wage on companies receiving business assistance from the city; the least common feature is for cities to impose the requirement on themselves, by covering city employees.

Advocates of living wage laws claim that they will help the poor, but critics argue that they will weaken the business climate and thus ultimately harm workers. This dispute reflects the likelihood that living wage laws help some workers and families (those who experience wage gains and do not face employment declines) and hurt others (those who face reduced employment prospects). No one seriously disputes that these tradeoffs exist; rather, the argument hinges on the size of the gains or the losses to low-wage workers and low-income families.

Given the prominence and (growing) scope of the living wage movement, it is critical to analyze the effects of these laws on low-wage workers and poor families to enable policymakers, employers, labor unions, and voters to make informed judgments regarding the merits of this policy innovation. The research presented in this monograph represents the first systematic attempt to assess evidence on the actual effects of living wage laws, looking at changes in the economic fortunes of individuals and families in cities that passed living wage laws, in comparison with similar workers, over the same period, in cities that did not implement living wages. There are three main sets of findings.

Effects on Wages of Low-Wage Workers

On average, there are sizable positive effects of living wage ordinances on the wages of low-wage workers in the cities in which these ordinances are enacted. At the same time, the magnitudes of the estimated wage effects are larger than would be expected given the limited coverage of city contractors by the most common type of living wage law. Rather, the large wage effects are driven by cities in which the coverage of living wage laws is broader—namely, cities that impose living wages on employers receiving business assistance from the city. Thus, existing analyses of the likely effects of living wage laws based on narrow coverage of city contractors, and ignoring business assistance provisions, may be quite misleading. At least some living wage ordinances— specifically those with business assistance provisions—may to some extent operate more like broader minimum wage laws than like narrow living wage laws centered on city contractors and perhaps city employees.

The Effects of Living Wage Laws on Low-Wage Workers and Low-Income Families

Although living wage laws raise the wages of low-wage workers, they also appear to reduce employment among the affected workers, with these negative effects arising concurrently with wage increases. These disemployment effects counter the positive effect of living wage laws on the wages of low-wage workers, pointing to the tradeoff between wages and employment that economic theory would predict.

Economic theory offers some guidance as to the expected employment tradeoff, but it makes no prediction regarding the effect of living wage laws on poverty. The effect ultimately depends on the family incomes of workers who experience wage gains and individuals who experience reduced employment prospects. The empirical analysis provides some evidence that living wage ordinances result in moderate reductions in the likelihood that urban families live in poverty.

Do Narrow Living Wage Laws Offer Gains to Unionized Municipal Workers?

Aside from offering benefits to low-wage workers and low-income families, living wage laws may reduce the incentives for cities to contract out work that would otherwise be done by municipal employees, hence increasing the bargaining power of municipal unions and leading to higher wages. Indeed narrow living wage laws may generate this latter effect without delivering benefits to low-wage workers and low-income families generally. Labor unions representing municipal workers are, in fact, very active in the movement to pass living wage laws. More directly, the evidence indicates that the wages of unionized municipal workers are increased as a result of narrow, contractor-only living wages—the same narrow living wage laws for which no beneficial effects for low-wage workers and low-income families are detected. Thus, although there may be other reasons why narrow living wage laws are passed—including, for example, political feasibility—the gains these laws generate for unionized municipal workers may provide a partial explanation.

Summary

The research presented in this monograph leads to a number of conclusions, and what one takes away as its primary "lessons" is likely to depend in part on one's perspective on or role in the debate over living wages. The finding that living wage laws indeed have their most "direct" intended consequence—raising the wages of low-wage workers—is likely to encourage policymakers, whatever their own view of the merits of such laws. Standard economic theory—which predicts that, whatever their other benefits, living wage laws should lead to some tradeoffs in the form of lower employment—receives some support. Those who work on behalf of living wage laws as a means of reducing urban poverty should be heartened by the evidence suggesting that living wage laws may help to achieve this goal. Finally, those who skeptically suggest that unions may support living wage laws not out of beneficence toward the lowest-wage workers, but rather to reap gains for unionized municipal workers, may find their skepticism reinforced by evidence that the latter appears to occur.

In interpreting this evidence, though, it is important to realize that these different conclusions are not necessarily in conflict. Living wage laws can in principle engender some employment losses, but coupled with wage increases, and depending on the magnitude and distribution of each of these, help the poor. And higher-wage unionized municipal workers can gain at the same time that low-income families gain.

A cautious reading of the evidence, then, suggests that, on net, living wages may provide some assistance to the urban poor. But this by no means implies that living wages constitute the best method of combating urban poverty, in terms of cost-effectiveness or distributional effects. Policymakers contemplating implementing living wage laws, and policy analysts assessing living wage laws, should give full consideration to comparisons among different methods of reducing poverty, including various types of living wage laws and alternative policies altogether.[1]

Remaining Questions

This monograph has attempted to address a broad sweep of rather fundamental questions regarding living wage laws, including whether they have much effect at all, whether they achieve their main policy goal, and why cities pass living wage laws in the first place. But many important questions remain to be addressed before policy analysts should feel confident that they have a well-established set of findings on which to draw strong conclusions regarding living wages.

First, many pieces of the puzzle are not yet in place. The CPS data analyzed in this monograph provide representative samples of workers, individuals, and families from cities but scant information on how to distinguish workers most likely to be directly affected by living wage

---

[1]As an example, in 1999, after first considering a living wage proposal, Montgomery County, Maryland, opted instead for a local EITC.

laws. In particular, the CPS data are unable to identify with any certainty those workers covered by city contracts or working for employers receiving business assistance from the city. This limitation precludes empirical research regarding many of the interesting microeconomic consequences of living wage laws. For example, how does employment at covered employers respond? Does employment tend to flow from covered to uncovered sectors? Are the wages of covered and uncovered workers affected differently? Furthermore, how do employment adjustments take place? Do the reductions primarily take the form of existing employers downsizing, or do some employers relocate outside the city? Answers to these questions might help policymakers decide how to minimize the adverse effects of living wage laws. In addition, because the CPS data are at the level of the individual, as opposed to the level of the firm, they are unable to answer questions about how specific employers react to living wage laws, including questions such as whether wage spillovers occur across or within firms.

Second, institutional knowledge of the day-to-day workings of living wage laws is virtually nonexistent. The only exception is a study by Sander and Lokey (1998) on enforcement and compliance problems and solutions in a case study of the implementation of a living wage law in Los Angeles. Case studies of this nature are valuable in generating such institutional knowledge. However, there are as yet no systematic data on how cities implement living wage laws, resources devoted to enforcement, penalties for noncompliance, etc. In the absence of such information, it is impossible to address any questions relating to the best ways to implement living wage laws. Furthermore, evidence that the effects of living wage laws are stronger when enforcement is more vigorous and penalties more severe would bolster any conclusions regarding the causal effects of living wage laws that might be drawn from the present monograph.

Third, the evidence of union support for living wages and economic gains to unionized municipal workers suggests that more attention to the political economy of living wages may prove productive. In particular, it may be possible to model the determinants of the incidence and perhaps even the magnitudes of living wage laws. In addition to deepening understanding of the economic and political forces shaping the living wage movement, such research can also help in designing strategies to evaluate the effects of living wage laws.

Fourth, aside from the wage, employment, and income tradeoffs on which this monograph focuses, there are potential second-round effects of living wages that require study. Because living wages are local, employers may be able to avoid coverage by terminating contracts, grants, abatements, etc., with the city. If this occurs, fewer firms could be left to bid on city contracts, which might lead to less competitive bidding and therefore higher prices for city services. Aside from this, living wage laws may have an additional adverse consequence if some of the affected recipients of business assistance that subsequently withdraw or reduce services are nonprofit organizations providing services to needy individuals and families. In addition, if the higher costs imposed by living wages are absorbed by the cities passing these laws, higher city taxes or reduced services may result, with potentially negative consequences for taxpayers and property values. It remains for future empirical research to assess whether these second-round effects of living wages occur, their magnitudes, and on whom they fall.

Fifth, there are at the time of this writing unanswered questions about future developments in living wage campaigns. For example, although this monograph has offered a partial explanation as to why living wage laws often cover only city contractors, an increased emphasis on broader living wage laws would tend to undermine the view that these laws are principally designed to help unionized municipal workers, and vice versa. In addition, some states (to date Arizona, Colorado, Louisiana, Missouri, and Utah) have recently passed laws prohibiting localities from implementing minimum wages or living wages in excess of state minimum wages, and it remains to be seen how this potential struggle between state and local authorities plays out over the next few years.

Sixth, living wages and, even more so, research on living wages are to some extent both in their infancy. Living wages have been in existence only for a short time and as yet in a limited number of cities for more than a year or two. More work will need to be done to evaluate whether the evidence of wage gains, employment declines, and decreases in poverty hold in a larger sample of cities that have adopted such legislation over a longer period of time. In addition, given the very high levels of some recently passed living wages, more refined analyses of how these effects vary with the level of the living wage (and local wages and prices) are critical. Future research will help to determine just how solid a basis there is for drawing conclusions regarding the effects of living wages, by revealing how robust the findings are to other reasonable research strategies.

Finally, the limitations discussed to this point focus in large part on refinements to the analysis of the effects of living wages on low-wage workers and low-income families. There are also other issues essential to a full-scale policy evaluation, including the effects of living wages on municipal budgets; the extent to which higher labor costs are absorbed by contractors or instead passed through to cities; the consequences of living wages for the provision of city services, stemming from budgetary considerations or effects of living wages on productivity; the equity effects of living wage laws (including their effects on women and minorities); and the effects of living wages on overall economic welfare.

In and of itself, the evidence presented in this monograph does not lead to a concrete policy recommendation regarding living wages. However, by finding some evidence that living wages do have a positive effect on wages at the bottom end of the wage distribution and also appear to lead to modest poverty reductions (despite some employment loss), it suggests that at least some of the beneficial claims of living wage advocates are borne out in the data. This suggests that other potential costs and benefits of living wages should be explored to attempt to arrive at an overall assessment of the policy, recognizing that the evaluation may well differ depending on the local economy and the specific law considered. Only with a full accounting of the costs and benefits will policymakers, employer organizations, labor unions, and voters be in a position to make informed judgments regarding the merits of this increasingly popular policy innovation.

References

Alunan, Susan, et al., *The Living Wage in San Francisco: Analysis of Economic Impact, Administrative, and Policy Issues*, San Francisco Urban Institute, San Francisco, California, 1999.

Ashenfelter, Orley, and Robert S. Smith, "Compliance with the Minimum Wage Law," *Journal of Political Economy,* Vol. 87, No. 2, April 1979, pp. 333–350.

Bertrand, Marianne, Esther Duflo, and Sendhil Mullainathan, "How Much Should We Trust Differences-in-Differences Estimates?" Mimeograph, University of Chicago, Chicago, Illinois, 2001.

Besley, Timothy, and Anne Case, "Unnatural Experiments? Estimating the Incidence of Endogenous Policies," *The Economic Journal,* Vol. 110, 2000, pp. F672–694.

Bhattacharyya, Arunava, and Elliott Parker, "An Examination of the Effect of Ownership on the Relative Efficiency of Public and Private Water Utilities," *Land Economics,* Vol. 70, No. 2, May 1994, pp. 197–209.

Brock, William A., and Stephen P. Magee, "The Economics of Special Interest Politics: The Case of the Tariff," *American Economic Review Papers and Proceedings*, Vol. 68, 1978, pp. 246–250.

Brown, Charles, Curtis Gilroy, and Andrew Kohen, "Time Series Evidence on the Effect of the Minimum Wage on Youth Employment and Unemployment," *Journal of Human Resources,* Vol. 18, No. 1, 1983, pp. 3–31.

Brown, Charles, Curtis Gilroy, and Andrew Kohen, "The Effect of the Minimum Wage on Employment and Unemployment," *Journal of Economic Literature*, Vol. 20, 1982, pp. 487–528.

Bureau of the Census, *CPS Technical Paper 63: Design & Methodology*, Bureau of the Census, Washington, D.C., 1997.

Burkhauser, Richard V., Kenneth A. Couch, and David C. Wittenburg, "A Reassessment of the New Economics of the Minimum Wage Literature with Monthly Data from the Current Population Survey," *Journal of Labor Economics*, Vol. 18, No. 4, October 2000, pp. 653–680.

Burkhauser, Richard V., Kenneth A. Couch, and David C. Wittenburg, "'Who Gets What' from Minimum Wage Hikes: A Re-Estimation of Card and Krueger's Distributional Analysis in Myth and Measurement: The New Economics of the Minimum Wage," *Industrial and Labor Relations Review*, Vol. 49, No. 3, April 1996, pp. 547–552.

Card, David, and Alan B. Krueger, *Myth and Measurement: The New Economics of the Minimum Wage*, Princeton University Press, Princeton, New Jersey, 1995.

Card, David, and Alan B. Krueger, "Minimum Wages and Employment: A Case Study of the Fast-Food Industry in New Jersey and Pennsylvania," *American Economic Review*, Vol. 84, 1994, pp. 772–793.

Employment Policies Institute, *The Employment Impact of a Comprehensive Living Wage Law: Evidence from California*, Employment Policies Institute, Washington, D.C., 1999.

Employment Policies Institute, *The Baltimore Study: Omissions, Fabrications, and Flaws*, Employment Policies Institute, Washington, D.C., 1998.

Fishback, Price V., and Shawn Everett Kantor, "The Political Economy of Workers' Compensation Benefit Levels, 1910–1930," *Explorations in Economic History*, Vol. 35, 1998, pp. 109–139.

Fuchs, Victor R., Alan B. Krueger, and James M. Poterba, "Economists' Views About Parameters, Values, and Policies: Survey Results in

Labor and Public Economics," *Journal of Economic Literature,* Vol. 36, 1998, pp. 1387–1425.

Golan, Amos, Jeffrey M. Perloff, and Ximing Wu, "Welfare Effects of Minimum Wage and Other Government Policies," Mimeograph, University of California, Berkeley, California, 2001.

Goldin, Claudia, "The Political Economy of Immigration Restrictions in the United States, 1890–1921," in Claudia Goldin and Gary D. Libecap, eds., *The Regulated Economy,* University of Chicago Press, Chicago, Illinois, 1994, pp. 223–257.

Gramlich, Edward M., "Impact of Minimum Wages on Other Wages, Employment, and Family Incomes," *Brookings Papers on Economic Activity,* No. 2, 1976, pp. 409–451.

Grossman, Jean Baldwin, "The Impact of the Minimum Wage on Other Wages," *Journal of Human Resources,* Vol. 18, No. 3, Summer 1983, pp. 359–378.

Hamermesh, Daniel S., *Labor Demand,* Princeton University Press, Princeton, New Jersey, 1993.

Heckman, James, "Sample Selection Bias as a Specification Error," *Econometrica,* Vol. 47, No. 1, 1979, pp. 153–161.

Hollas, Daniel R., and Stanley R. Stansell, "The Economic Efficiency of Public vs. Private Gas Distribution Utilities," *Annals of Public and Cooperative Economics,* Vol. 65, No. 2, 1994, pp. 281–300.

Kessler, Daniel P., and Lawrence Katz, "Prevailing Wage Laws and Construction Labor Markets," NBER Working Paper No. 7454, Cambridge, Massachusetts, 1999.

Kezdi, Gabor, "Robust Standard Error Estimation in Fixed-Effects Panel Models," Mimeograph, University of Michigan, Ann Arbor, Michigan, 2001.

Kubik, Jeffrey D., and John R. Moran, "Can Policy Changes Be Treated as Natural Experiments? Evidence from State Excise Taxes," Mimeograph, Syracuse University, Syracuse, New York, 2001.

Kuo-Ping, Chang, and Pei-Hua Kao, "The Relative Efficiency of Public versus Private Municipal Bus Firms: An Application of Data Envelopment Analysis," *Journal of Productivity Analysis,* Vol. 3, No. 1–2, June 1992, pp. 67–84.

Leibenstein, Harvey, "On the Basic Proposition of X-Efficiency Theory," *American Economic Review,* Vol. 68, No. 2, May 1978, pp. 328–332.

Meyer, Bruce, and Dan Rosenbaum, "Welfare, the Earned Income Tax Credit, and the Labor Supply of Single Mothers," NBER Working Paper No. 7363, Cambridge, Massachusetts, 1999.

Mincer, Jacob, "Unemployment Effects of Minimum Wages," *Journal of Political Economy,* Vol. 84, No. 4, Pt. 2, 1976, pp. S87–S104.

Mood, Alexander, Franklin A. Graybill, and Duane C. Boes, *Introduction to the Theory of Statistics,* McGraw-Hill Book Company, New York, 1974.

Moulton, Brent R., "Random Group Effects and the Precision of Regression Estimates," *Journal of Econometric,* Vol. 32, 1986, pp. 385–397.

Neumark, David, and Scott Adams, "Detecting Effects of Living Wage Laws," Mimeograph, Public Policy Institute of California, San Francisco, California, 2001a.

Neumark, David, and Scott Adams, "Do Living Wage Ordinances Reduce Urban Poverty?" Mimeograph, Public Policy Institute of California, San Francisco, California, 2001b.

Neumark, David, and William Wascher, "Do Minimum Wages Fight Poverty?" Forthcoming in *Economic Inquiry.*

Neumark, David, and William Wascher, "Using the EITC to Help Poor Families: New Evidence and a Comparison with the Minimum Wage," *National Tax Journal,* Vol. LIV, No. 2, 2001, pp. 281–317.

Neumark, David, and William Wascher, "Minimum Wages and Employment: A Case Study of the Fast-Food Industry in New

Jersey and Pennsylvania: Comment," *American Economic Review,* Vol. 90, No. 5, 2000, pp. 1362–1396.

Neumark, David, and William Wascher, "Reconciling the Evidence on Employment Effects of Minimum Wages—A Review of Our Research Findings," in Marvin Kosters, ed., *The Effects of the Minimum Wage on Employment,* American Enterprise Institute, Washington, D.C., 1996, pp. 55–86.

Neumark, David, and William Wascher, "Employment Effects of Minimum and Subminimum Wages: Panel Data on State Minimum Wage Laws," *Industrial and Labor Relations Review,* Vol. 46, No. 1, 1992, pp. 55–81.

Neumark, David, Mark Schweitzer, and William Wascher, "Minimum Wage Effects Throughout the Wage Distribution," Mimeograph, Michigan State University, East Lansing, Michigan, 1999.

Neumark, David, Mark Schweitzer, and William Wascher, "The Effects of Minimum Wages on the Distribution of Family Incomes: A Non-Parametric Analysis," NBER Working Paper No. 6536, Cambridge, Massachusetts, 1998.

Niedt, Christopher, Greg Ruiters, Dana Wise, and Erica Schoenberger, "The Effects of the Living Wage in Baltimore," Economic Policy Institute Working Paper No. 119, Washington, D.C., 1999.

Nissen, Bruce, "The "Social Movement" Dynamics of Living Wage Campaigns," Mimeograph, Florida International University, Miami, Florida, 2000.

O'Brien-Strain, Margaret, and Thomas MaCurdy, *Increasing the Minimum Wage: California's Winners and Losers,* Public Policy Institute of California, San Francisco, California, 2000.

Pollin, Robert, and Mark Brenner, *Economic Analysis of Santa Monica Living Wage Proposal,* Political Economy Research Institute, University of Massachusetts, Amherst, Massachusetts, 2000.

Pollin, Robert, and Stephanie Luce, *The Living Wage: Building a Fair Economy*, The New Press, New York, 1998.

Reich, Michael, and Peter Hall, *Living Wages at the Airport and Port of San Francisco*, Institute of Industrial Relations: Bay Area Living Wage Research Group, Berkeley, California, 1999.

Reich, Michael, Peter Hall, and Fiona Hsu, *Living Wages and the San Francisco Economy: The Benefits and the Costs*, Center on Pay and Inequality, University of California, Berkeley, California, 1999.

Reynolds, David, *Impact of Detroit's Living Wage Law on Non-Profit Organizations*, Detroit: Center for Urban Studies and Labor Studies Center, Wayne State University, Detroit, Michigan, 2000.

Reynolds, David, *The Impact of the Detroit Living Wage Ordinance*, Center for Urban Studies and Labor Studies Center, Wayne State University, Detroit, Michigan, 1999.

Sander, Richard, and Sean Lokey, *The Los Angeles Living Wage: The First Eighteen Months*, UCLA and the Fair Housing Institute, Los Angeles, California, 1998.

Sander, Richard H., E. Douglass Williams, and Joseph Doherty, *An Economic Analysis of the Proposed Santa Monica Living Wage*, Empirical Research Group, UCLA, Los Angeles, California, 2000.

Sen, Amartya, *On Economic Inequality*, Clarendon Press, Oxford, United Kingdom (Expanded Edition), 1997.

Shaviro, Daniel, *Effective Marginal Tax Rates on Low-Income Households*, Employment Policies Institute, Washington, D.C., 1999.

Tolley, George, Peter Bernstein, and Michael D. Lesage, *Economic Analysis of a Living Wage Ordinance*, Employment Policies Institute, Washington, D.C., 1999.

Weisbrot, Mark, and Michelle Sforza-Roderick, *Baltimore's Living Wage Law: An Analysis of the Fiscal and Economic Costs of Baltimore City Ordinance 442*, The Preamble Center for Public Policy, Washington, D.C., 1996.

Williams, E. Douglass, and Richard H. Sander, *An Empirical Analysis of the Proposed Los Angeles Living Wage Ordinance*, Mimeograph, Carleton College, Northfield, Minnesota, 1997.

Williams, Regina, *Analysis of a Living Wage Policy*, City Manager's Published Report, San Jose, California, 1998.

Zabin, Carol, Michael Reich, and Peter Hall, *Living Wages at the Port of Oakland*, Center for Labor Research and Education, University of California, Berkeley, California, 1999.

Zavodny, Madeline, "The Effect of the Minimum Wage on Employment and Hours," *Labour Economics,* Vol. 7, No. 6, November, 2000, pp. 729–750.

About the Author

DAVID NEUMARK

David Neumark is a professor of economics at Michigan State University and a research associate at the National Bureau of Economic Research. He specializes in research on labor market policy, working in such areas as age and sex discrimination, school-to-work transitions, the supplemental security income program, and affirmative action. His research has been supported by the National Science Foundation, the National Institute on Aging, the National Cancer Institute, the Russell Sage Foundation, and the U.S. Departments of Education and Labor. He has written most extensively on minimum wages, initially focusing on disemployment effects, and currently is studying the effects of minimum wages on income distribution. He holds a Ph.D. in economics from Harvard University.

Other Related PPIC Publications

California's Rising Income Inequality: Causes and Concerns
Deborah Reed

The Distribution of Income in California
Deborah Reed, Melissa Glenn Haber, Laura Mameesh

"Poverty in California: Levels, Trends, and Demographic Dimensions"
California Counts: Population Trends and Profiles
Volume 3, Number 3, November 2001
Deborah Reed, Richard Van Swearingen

Increasing the Minimum Wage: California's Winners and Losers
Margaret O'Brien-Strain, Thomas MaCurdy

PPIC publications may be ordered by phone or from our website
(800) 232-5343 [mainland U.S.]
(415) 291-4400 [Canada, Hawaii, overseas]
www.ppic.org

DATE DUE

DEC 01 2003			
NOV 1 9 2003		JUN 0 2 REC'D	
iLL 3713285/47716 4/10/04		OhioLINK	
APR 1 5 REC'D		AUG 2 5 REC'D	
		OCT 1 6 2006	
		OCT 2 0 REC'D	
MAY 0 8 2006		MAR 1 9 2007	
MAY 0 7 REC'D		MAR 1 5 REC'D	
OhioLINK			
MAY 1 2 REC'D			
DEC 1 2 2005 RETD FIRE	DEC 1 4 2005		
DEC 1 5 REC'D			
APR 1 3 2006			

GAYLORD
PRINTED IN U.S.A.